# OUTDOORS
# WITH GOD

# OUTDOORS
# WITH GOD

*Devotional Thoughts*

*on the Great Outdoors*

## LANCE MOORE

BARBOUR
PUBLISHING

ISBN 1-58660-919-X

Published by Barbour Publishing, Inc., P.O. Box 719, Uhrichsville, Ohio 44683, www.barbourpublishing.com

*Our mission is to publish and distribute inspirational products offering exceptional value and biblical encouragement to the masses.*

 Member of the
Evangelical Christian
Publishers Association

Printed in the United States of America.
5 4 3 2

# CONTENTS

Introduction . . . . . . . . . . . . . . . . . . . . . . . . . . . . . . . . 9

1. My Father the Fisherman . . . . . . . . . . . . . . . . . . . 11
2. God of the Water . . . . . . . . . . . . . . . . . . . . . . . . . 21
3. God and the Fish . . . . . . . . . . . . . . . . . . . . . . . . . 31
4. Fish and Snakes . . . . . . . . . . . . . . . . . . . . . . . . . . 41
5. In the Garden . . . . . . . . . . . . . . . . . . . . . . . . . . . 51
6. God and the Quiet Hunter . . . . . . . . . . . . . . . . . . 57
7. God as the Hunter (Part One) . . . . . . . . . . . . . . . 63
8. God as the Hunter (Part Two) . . . . . . . . . . . . . . . 73
9. God and the Birds of the Air . . . . . . . . . . . . . . . . 81
10. The Camouflage of God . . . . . . . . . . . . . . . . . . . . 89
11. Something Dark in the Woods . . . . . . . . . . . . . . . 97
12. In King David's Camp . . . . . . . . . . . . . . . . . . . . 107
13. In Jacob's Camp . . . . . . . . . . . . . . . . . . . . . . . . . 117
14. Camping with Jesus . . . . . . . . . . . . . . . . . . . . . . 125
15. Cookout with Jesus . . . . . . . . . . . . . . . . . . . . . . . 133
16. The Spiritual Journey (Part One) . . . . . . . . . . . . 141
17. The Spiritual Journey (Part Two) . . . . . . . . . . . . 149
18. The Calm of the Green . . . . . . . . . . . . . . . . . . . . 157
19. In the Valley of Shadows . . . . . . . . . . . . . . . . . . 165
20. On the Mountaintop . . . . . . . . . . . . . . . . . . . . . . 173
21. Grandpa Mik's Shrimp Boat . . . . . . . . . . . . . . . 183
22. Boating Buddies . . . . . . . . . . . . . . . . . . . . . . . . . 191
23. God and the Fishermen: Back to Fishing . . . . . . . 199
24. Sinking Boats and a Titanic Question . . . . . . . . . 205
25. The Final Chapter? . . . . . . . . . . . . . . . . . . . . . . . 213

*Dedicated to my father, Bob Moore, a fisherman.*

*Thanks to Tom Butts, Lee Hough,*
*and Michael Warden for editorial assistance;*
*Peggy Blankenship and Diana Moore for proofreading.*

# INTRODUCTION

*by Dr. Thomas Lane Butts Jr.*

Preacher, I feel closer to God when I'm in the woods (or on the lake, or on the golf course) than I do in church." Every pastor has heard that excuse from parishioners as they explain their absence from church during hunting season or any Sunday that the weather permits outside sports. It's hard to argue against because it's true. God, who created the beauty of the rivers and forests, certainly does *seem* more present when we are surrounded by the great outdoors rather than confined to a hard church pew, wearing the least comfortable clothes in our wardrobe.

The Bible teaches that God is *always* present with us—even when we are not aware. Experiencing the presence of God in nature is a wonderful emotion. But feelings can be deceiving. To develop a vital faith, we need much more than a "warm, fuzzy feeling." What we sometimes call "Mother Nature"—God's handiwork—shows us only a part of *God's nature*, God's whole being and character. A faith that can be counted on in life and in death comes from a sense of community with other people, something we find in the company of Christians as we worship together on Sundays and as we share our lives together during the week. As a pastor myself, I hope that whatever you gain from Dr. Moore's book and from your time in the great outdoors will be only a portion of a well-rounded faith that includes an active life in the church.

Still, seeking God in the outdoors and marveling at the beauty of His creation can soothe and inspire the soul. This outdoor meditative tradition can be found in the best of the Bible and Christian history. King David wrote many psalms out in the wilds; St. Francis of Assisi expressed feelings of kinship with the sun, moon, stars, sky, trees, and animals; even Jesus often found it essential to withdraw "by boat privately to a solitary place" (Matthew 14:13).

"Tuning in" to God while immersed in creation is a means to significant spiritual growth. This does not come automatically. It requires paying attention. It demands observation. It calls for an intentional awareness of God's presence. Spiritual growth happens best when we recognize that God is with us always.

This book is not offered as a daily devotional; there are ample resources for that elsewhere. Instead, read this short book slowly. Read one lesson a week as a spark to get your mind and spirit focused on God as you head outdoors. Make this book a kind of "spiritual wake-up call." Bring it with you on camping or hunting trips, along with your Bible, as a visible reminder of your desire to encounter God wherever you go.

And remember, whether you are seated in a boat, a deer stand, or a church pew, Jesus said, "I am with you always. . . ."

# CHAPTER 1:

# MY FATHER THE FISHERMAN

TODAY'S SCRIPTURE:

*So God created the great creatures of the sea and*

*every living and moving thing with which the water teems,*

*according to their kinds, and every winged bird according*

*to its kind. And God saw that it was good.*

GENESIS 1:21

# FEAR OF FISHING

As a child, great moments of laughter, joy—and fear—came from fishing with my father. He propelled his three sons out into the rough waters of Mobile Bay in an old, flimsy sixteen-foot boat with an 18-horse Evinrude and all-too-much faith in moldy beat-up life jackets.

We would fish for saltwater trout until we boys grew bored for lack of a nibble. Then Dad would let us put some cut bait on the line, drop the hooks deep, and catch crabs. Actually, the crabs were catching us—they were never hooked; they simply were so greedy for the bait, they never relaxed their claw-grip, and we'd pull them into an ice chest.

On several occasions, the bloody crab lines attracted small sharks. I actually managed to hook one and bring it all the way up to the boat. While pulling the shark from the sea, I felt no pride, only *fear*. It dawned on me, even at the age of eight, that if our boat sank, I would not drown; I would become bait!

Fear tastes like salt water.

# THE JOY

The joy came in long, quiet hours spent with my father, who made his living as a pastor but in his heart was a fisherman. Alone on the water, just "us guys," it was the one time he might tell us bawdy jokes or share embarrassing tales from his own childhood. Interspersed with the crude laughter were also deep theological talks—not preachy lectures, but open and relaxed times when we boys could ask Dad the hard questions of life, death, and religion and not receive the easy platitudes often heard in sermons. The mixture of the holy and the profane, like the mix of joy and fear, made fishing a microcosm of human life.

Twenty years later, my seminary professor would say, "Nothing runs unmingled." I understood. In this life, joy and pain are two sides of the same coin; baptisms and funerals happen in the same sanctuary, sometimes on the same day. Although we try to compartmentalize our religion, the "secular" workaday world is carried with us in our pockets and purses of worries as we amble into pews on Sunday. And hopefully, the sacred stuff of God goes with us as we pour out of the church doors at noon toward our Evinrudes.

# SACRED BEAUTY

When we are outdoors (fishing, for example), the beauty of it all should remind us that God made this wider world, sharks and all. Creation is God's temple, and it is not neatly divided into "things sacred" versus "things secular." The things we deem holy, such as altar candles, brass crosses, stained-glass windows, are only dim representations of the true sacrament, which is "the earth and all that is in it" (Revelation 10:6).

When God made the world, each step of the way He paused, considered it, and "saw that it was good." Why does the first chapter of Genesis repeat this phrase, like a mantra, six times? God's handiwork—the natural world—reflects His own good nature. This is what the word "sacrament" means: a physical reminder of God's goodness and grace, symbolized by such mundane things as bread, wine, and water.

## JESUS THE FISHERMAN

That is why, when the Lord came to live on our planet, He became a common fisherman. Oh yes, I know Jesus was by trade first a carpenter and then (like my dad) a traveling preacher. But in His heart I believe Jesus was also a fisherman. He seemed to enjoy boats, even using one as a podium from which to preach to the crowd. He often taught His disciples in the midst of their fishing expeditions. After His resurrection, we don't find Jesus at the temple or at First Church, Galilee. We see Him on the shore, yelling directions to the fishermen about where they can catch the most fish! Jesus chose to hang out with the salty, rough-edged workingmen. He never shied away from the coarser side of life.

As we ponder this inseparable mixture in God's world of holy and profane, good and not so good, we can better appreciate the wisdom of His choice to come to planet Earth in the flesh. How else would God reach us, now that things are all mixed up—saints and sinners, priests and prostitutes, Pharisees and fishermen *all in the same boat?*

# A Calculated Gamble

God did something like what my dad did with an old gambler named Buford.[1] Buford had given up a life as a professional "cardsharp" in order to marry and settle down, but he was still known in the community as a rough character who would never attend church. Dad, knowing that Buford could not be easily persuaded to enter the realm of stained glass and fancy Sunday apparel, invited the gambler to go fishing. He accepted.

So the preacher and the gambler set out to catch fish. They first tried to tie the boat to an overhanging tree limb at a shallow fishing spot on Fish River, but the tree harbored a large wasp nest. They managed to escape with only a few wasp stings and decided to move to deeper water. After anchoring, the two settled in and caught a few white trout while my dad gently and casually spoke to Buford about God's love and of what it means to be a Christian. Suddenly, a dragonfly landed on Dad's wrist, in which hand he held a new rod and reel. With wasps on the mind, Dad instinctively waved his hands in a panic to shake off the bug, and the rod and reel went overboard! An exclamation that was not exactly holy came from Dad's lips, and Buford could barely contain his laughter over the sight of this panicking, cursing preacher losing his new rod.

Buford decided then and there that perhaps he, too, could become a Christian, by the same grace that covered a cussing preacher. The world of religion and church, which had seemed far removed from Buford's "other-side-of-the-tracks" experience, now appeared closer. Even an old sinning gambler like him could fit in with this man who was probably no more perfect as a preacher than he was as a cursing, fumbling fisherman. Buford understood something new about God's grace that day.

# GOD'S NET

God, who made the wasps, the dragonflies, the fish, and Buford, has a plan for this messed-up world. God's plan is to keep as much of His "catch" as He can, throwing back as little as possible. My earthly father was a fisherman; our heavenly Father is a fisher, too. And Jesus said that the kingdom of God is like a broad net that pulls in "all kinds" (Matthew 13:47). God is a "fisher of men," who patiently wades into rough waters to catch us all up in His nets of grace and love. So when you head out into the blue waters, think about your Father the Great Fisher, how He created this wonderful, stormy world as a sacrament for all of us. Contemplate how good it is that God does not sit only in church pews but also on boat seats with saints and rough-necks, in smooth water and rough seas. Be thankful that God searches those waters for things worth catching and keeping—like you and me.

TODAY'S PRAYER:

*O Lord, catch me up out of life's troubled waters into Your net of love. Forgive me for my failings—don't throw me back. And help me, in turn, to forgive those who act more like sinners than saints. In Christ's name. Amen.*

# Chapter 2:

# God of the Water

Today's Scripture:

*Jesus answered, "Everyone who drinks this water will be thirsty again, but whoever drinks the water I give him will never thirst. Indeed, the water I give him will become in him a spring of water welling up to eternal life."*

John 4:13–14

# Amazing Wet Stuff

Water. I am surrounded by it. I'm sitting on the dock of the bay, watching the tide roll away, just like Otis Redding; and I'm thinking about this liquid chameleon called water.

God's best invention has to be water. Such amazing stuff: strikingly beautiful in all its changing colors and all its variable forms, whether it be a gentle autumn shower, a winter crystalline snowfall, a delicate spring dew on flowers, or the summer sun reflected on the millions of gallons that make up Wolf Bay—where I now wade. A few degrees colder, and all this water turns as solid as a mountain. A few degrees hotter, and it all steams away. At room temperature, its liquid form sustains all living things; my own body is a big sack of bones and water.

Ice and steam and liquid, it's all the same miraculous combination of two hydrogen atoms and one oxygen, which when separated burn with ferocity, but bonded together extinguish fires. Water is the grand paradox. Water carries the heaviest steel battleship yet remains as tender and soft as a newborn baby in a bath. I imagine God kinda chuckled when He came up with this contradiction called *water*.

# Talking and Walking on Water

*S*o it is no wonder that Jesus was enthralled with water. He began His ministry in the Jordan River, covered in the stuff. His first miracle was turning water into a nice Merlot. He preached at the water's edge. He even walked on the water!

Jesus also used water as an "object lesson." A thirsty Jesus sat by a city well talking with a promiscuous Samaritan woman. She was not satisfied with her love life or with life in general. She brought Jesus a drink of water from the well, and in gratitude He spoke to the pain of her empty existence. "The water I give. . .will become. . .a spring of water welling up to eternal life." Jesus understood that water is essential to physical life. It quenches, cleanses, nourishes, and satisfies better than any cola. He also understood that water, being the essence of our physical beings, is a fitting metaphor for the longings of our spiritual selves. Our spoiled and promiscuous generation, even more than that of the Samaritan woman, is thirsty for *something*, lusting after satisfaction but never seeming to find it. Water, water, everywhere, yet not a drop to drink.

# Water in the Bible

The Bible is filled with hundreds of references to water, fountains, and rivers, half the time meaning physical streams and rivers but the rest alluding to divine water, such as in Revelation 7:17: " 'He will lead them to springs of living water.' " Although we long for those springs, we have a problem—spiritual water is invisible. We have difficulty picturing this Unseen Spirit and unseen drink. The Bible suggests that a starting point may be to meditate upon visible, earthly rivers as we try to understand more about the divine streams of living (spiritual) water. Do that with me for a moment.

From here on Wolf Bay, one can travel by boat not many miles to Fish River, where I grew up. Fish River is a rippled mirror of deep forest greens and sky blues, a mixture of shady and sunny, shallows and depths. When I was a toddler, we could ride for hours in our slow boat—like Bogart on the *African Queen*—without seeing much more than a few shabby cabins, mostly hidden by the thickets and trees, camouflaged behind copious Spanish moss. It isn't an exciting river—no falls or rapids or mountain walls—but it runs wide and deep and strong, a proud parent to a shoving crowd of cedars, oaks, pines, ferns, and vines lined up on the banks, stretching and clawing with naked roots to drink.

The river gave drink to every living thing.

Picturing Fish River in my mind helps me engage Bible passages such as Psalm 1:3: "He is like a tree planted by streams of water, which yields its fruit in season and whose leaf does not wither."

# WATER IN THE DESERT

The people of Jesus' time and place had no trouble envisioning the life-giving power of waters and rivers. Living in a desert, they saw vividly how rivers brought a fecundity of flora and fauna to their otherwise dry and barren land. The Jordan River runs through the desert of the Holy Land and through the narrative of the Old and New Testaments. The metaphorical "stream" that connects Genesis, the Psalms, the Gospels, and the Book of Revelation is a single holy river, the Divine River of Life, a spiritual spring that flows from God into our thirsty souls, bringing us life abundant and life eternal. It is featured in the climax of the biblical story. "Then the angel showed me the river of the water of life, as clear as crystal, flowing from the throne of God and of the Lamb" (Revelation 22:1). Jesus was bold enough to suggest that He was the source of that fountain of life and that He could be as life-giving to the human spirit as the city well was to the thirsty Samaritan woman.

# DEAD FISH AND LIVING WATERS

To connect us again to our theme of "fishing," consider this: When you remove a fish from the water, it can stay alive for an hour or so. Then it dies. Think of that fish as your soul. Removed from the living water of Christ, you might stay alive for awhile—for a hundred years at most, you could remain physically alive. But eventually, your spiritual self, your soul, would wither up and die. A man without Christ is, as the saying goes, "like a fish out of water."

In the movie *A River Runs Through It,* a Presbyterian minister teaches his two sons deep spiritual truths as they fly-fish alongside the Big Blackfoot River. As the water gurgles over smooth pebbles and jagged rocks, the father tells his sons something like this, "Beneath the water are stones that have been here for thousands of years, but beneath them are the eternal words of God." Very poetic. But in real life, the boys would have likely replied, "What the heck are you talking about?" And I doubt the Samaritan woman really understood everything Jesus was saying about a "spring welling up inside you to eternal life." He reached her not at an intellectual level so much as in the heart and soul. She was lonely. She was longing for meaning and fulfillment inside. As Jesus sipped the cool water she had handed Him, He was able to touch her at the inmost level, deep down at the point of her spiritual drought. Christ became her "living water," flowing through her heart and mind, the source of satisfaction in her thirsty life.

Like poetry, we don't have to *fully* understand the symbolism of water, or the words of Jesus to the woman, or the metaphorical words of the Presbyterian minister to his sons about the river. What we are called to do is open our minds, hearts, and spirits to God's life-giving presence in whatever form it comes to us: through nature, through prayer, through Bible study, through Christian fellowship. Just soak in all these words and images like a sponge—bathe in them, drink them in. Like water. Like spirit. Like God.

TODAY'S PRAYER:

*O God, who hovered over the waters of creation, bathe me in Your grace. Give me the inner spiritual spring that the longings of my soul may be quenched. O Jesus, who humbled Yourself in the Jordan River, wash me, cleanse me, forgive me, make me whole and satisfied, that I might one day reach Your heavenly River of Life. Amen.*

# Chapter 3:

# God and the Fish

Today's Scripture:

*But the Lord provided a great fish to swallow Jonah,*

*and Jonah was inside the fish three days and three nights.*

*From inside the fish Jonah prayed to the Lord his God.*

*He said: "In my distress I called to the Lord,*

*and he answered me. From the depths of the grave*

*I called for help, and you listened to my cry."*

Jonah 1:17–2:2

# FISH, MIRACLE AND MYSTERY

People love fishing for all kinds of reasons. Most, like my dad, are best described as "water-hunters," for they are in it for the hunt; like detectives deciphering the wind, the weather, and the location, they fish for the sheer pleasure of the chase. They truly love the fish themselves. Not just to eat. They see the beauty of the fish, the miracle of the fish; and in that appreciation, these anglers sense that fish represent something magically reflective of the mythical and the spiritual. Anyone who reads the Gospels already knows that fish have something to do with faith, and even nonfishers can learn something about Christ and the Resurrection from this meditation on fish.

God created the fish of the sea as one of His first and foremost accomplishments; and ever since, they have served as God's favorite symbols of the mystery of life and death. Fish are like life—teeming and shiny when young; rainbow colored on sunny days; unpredictable, bloody, and visceral when cut open. Fish are like death—wordless, quietly hidden in the shadows and depths, there even when we don't think about them being there. Fish are like God—usually unseen, glimpsed in short leaps, yet always present. They swim unattached and aimless in the vast ocean, just as dreams float about in our subconscious.

# Fish as Great Inventions

Consider what amazing contraptions fish are. Fish live at all depths of the ocean, crawl on the land, and glide through the air. Fish can swim as fast as boats, and whales can grow as big as ships. They surface, dive, submerge, and hover in the water with more agility than the most sophisticated submarine. This is a more difficult feat than one might imagine.

The first military submarine was not invented until late in history, during the Civil War. The *H. L. Hunley* was built by a Southerner of the same name and first tested in the very waters where my dad and I fish—Mobile Bay. It immediately sank and killed her first crew. The *Hunley* was salvaged, reengineered, and moved to the Atlantic Coast, where Mr. Hunley himself took command, promptly sinking the sub and killing yet another crew. The Confederates raised her again, tinkered some more, and launched the first successful attack by a submarine against a ship, after which the *Hunley* sank a third and final time. The point is, the ability to swim underwater for long periods is a most complex endeavor. Fish are, nautically speaking, smarter than humans. You might say that when God invented fish, He was just showing off.

Perhaps this is why God made the fish a symbol of the

Resurrection of Jesus. You have heard from childhood the grand story of "Jonah and the Whale"—actually, the Bible calls it "a great fish." Jesus took that story of the great fish and made it a sign of His passion, death, and His rising from the dead. Hear the story again in modern terms.

# Caught and Released

Before H. L. Hunley, Jonah was the first person to travel by submarine—a God-given submarine, not a man-made one. Otherwise, Jonah was a lot like you and me. When God asked him to go one way, Jonah ran the other. Jonah was "chicken." God had asked Jonah to go to the city of Nineveh and preach against that city's wickedness. I imagine that Jonah was already a preacher, serving a comfortable parish in his hometown. Life was good at First Church. The congregation loved Jonah, paid him well, and supplied him with a pleasant parsonage in the suburbs. He had a membership in the country club and was working on lowering his golf score. Then God spoke: Leave all this comfort and go make trouble in a foreign city. Who can blame Jonah for running?

Jonah continued his escape by ship until in the midst of a horrible storm his superstitious shipmates tossed him overboard. It would have been certain death if God had not intervened. He sent a "great fish" to swallow Jonah whole. Jonah survived in its belly for three days until it spit him up safely onto the shore. Humbled and in need of a bath, he relented and went to the people of Nineveh with the message of repentance as God had originally instructed. To his surprise, they received him well and the whole city repented.

Now ask yourself: Why did God contrive such an odd set of circumstances to save Jonah and the city of Nineveh?

Jesus gives us a partial answer. In Matthew 12:40, Jesus compared "the sign of Jonah" with His impending death and resurrection: " 'For as Jonah was three days and three nights in the belly of a huge fish, so the Son of Man [another title used for Christ] will be three days and three nights in the heart of the earth.' " God had used the great fish to save Jonah and Nineveh, *and,* indirectly, to save *us.* Jonah's fish provided a metaphor for salvation and a prophecy of the coming Christ. God included this weird "fish tale" in the Bible to point our attention to the message Jesus would bring about faith, resurrection, and the human reluctance to accept God's eternal plan.

# FISH AND FAITH

When you, O fisher-reader, after a long struggle with rod and reel, pull a fish from the waters, it is an electric moment, charged with a vitality of life. You and the fish are hooked—the fish with steel, the fisherman with adrenaline. Catching a fish feels like when a dream comes true, when some dim concept of the subconscious pops brightly into the real, waking world.

Faith is much like that. Faith begins as an almost imperceptible tug, then a murky image; and if we hold on long enough, faith comes into view as an active and living part of our lives. And when God becomes fully real to us—some call it "enlightenment," some call it "epiphany"—then faith is vivid and exciting.

Fishing is an act of faith. You cast the lure or bait out recklessly into the wideness of the river, you watch it sink out of sight, you gently whip and reel. . .and nothing happens. You pull it in and cast again. Seeing nothing, feeling nothing, you repeat this process again and again with the blind faith that the fish are there. If patient, you are rewarded with a sudden and unexpected pouncing of a fish against your bait, hook, and line. The rod bends with ferocity. Your adrenaline pumps as you begin the tug of war with the hidden fish. Sometimes the fish tantalizes you with a quick leap out of the water, into the air and sun, and then back down again into its private depths. After more patient action, you bring the fish to the surface and finally into the boat.

But it all started with *faith*.

Faith, like fishing, is a decision to pursue the unseen. Faith requires a conscious choice and action. Living without faith is like refusing to put bait on your hook and then wondering why it comes back empty. Living *with* faith is analogous to my dad's habit of buying expensive bait shrimp with the hope of catching better fish. Christian faith is a most outlandish hope for a better outcome—hope in "hooking the big one." But here the analogy breaks down, because the stakes are much higher with faith than with fishing. What we have the potential of catching is nothing less than eternal life!

# FISH AND RESURRECTION

In the next chapter, we will see how the first Greek "code symbol" for Christ's name was "fish." It seems that God has given us the fish as a sign pointing to resurrection. After rising from the tomb, what did Jesus first do for His disciples? He helped them net, cook, and eat an extravagant catch of fish. God's extravagance on behalf of sinners was shown with Jonah and the "great fish" that saved him from a watery grave. It continued with Jesus breaking two pieces of cooked fish to feed a crowd of over five thousand. It culminated in the resurrected Christ coming in person to the disciples as they fished by the Galilean shore. Yet none of this has meaning for us today unless we catch the reality of faith for ourselves. So read on. . .and keep fishing.

TODAY'S PRAYER:

*O Lord, help me do better than Jonah: to have the courage to face challenges, not run from them. Forgive me for my lack of faith. Every time I pull a fish from the water, remind me of the miracle of Life, that I might have stronger faith in the Resurrection. In Christ's name. Amen.*

# CHAPTER 4:

# FISH AND SNAKES

TODAY'S SCRIPTURES:

*Confessing their sins, they were baptized by [John]*

*in the Jordan River. But when he saw many of the*

*Pharisees and Sadducees coming to where he was baptizing,*

*he said to them: "You brood of vipers!"*

MATTHEW 3:6–7

*"Which of you fathers, if your son asks for a fish,*

*will give him a snake instead?"*

LUKE 11:11

# THE OPPOSITE OF FISH

On another boyhood fishing adventure with my dad, I caught something more frightening than a shark. My little rod and reel was not much more than a toy. The rod suddenly bent double. I gripped it tight in my seven-year-old hands and imagined I had hooked a trophy-sized speckled trout, our targeted prey in the bay that morning. But when I brought it up to the gunnel, to my horror, I saw not a fish, but a snake! My brother and I felt no comfort when my dad assured us that it was not a snake at all, but an eel. It looked and moved like a slimy, twisting snake, and as far as we were concerned, there was not room in the boat for both a sea serpent and us.

In Luke 11, Jesus spoke of a fish as a good gift from one's father and a serpent as an evil gift. From my eel-catching experience, I could see clearly how a snake can be understood to be the complete opposite of a fish. And it was comforting to learn that I was not alone in my aversion to snakes. Metaphorically speaking, God has a strong fondness for fish and an equal but opposite opinion of snakes. The Bible uses the words "serpent" and "vipers" to describe the devil and his slippery agents, the Pharisees.

# FISHY PHARISEES?

Just who were the Pharisees, and why did Jesus view them as evil?

Let us return to the story of Jonah and the whale for an answer. After God forgave the Ninevites of their wickedness, Jonah was resentful. They were not "the chosen people." They were not even *good* people. Jonah felt that God was being too lenient! God rebuked Jonah harshly for having forgotten so quickly the lesson of the great fish. God had forgiven and saved the rebellious Jonah. How could Jonah then be so harsh and judgmental of other sinners?

This foreshadowed what would happen in Jesus' day. The Pharisees, like Jonah, were religious people; and also like Jonah, they thought that God was being far too generous in dispensing grace and forgiveness. They were resentful that Jesus associated with the tax collectors, prostitutes, winebibbers, and other "sinners." They wanted to reserve heaven for perfect people, which, in their arrogant view of reality, they defined as themselves. The leading Pharisees eventually conspired to kill Jesus because they could not accept His message of grace. Instead of loving and forgiving, they judged and condemned. They cared more about laws than about hearts. These cold-blooded elitists had a twisted—shall we say serpentine—notion of spirituality and religion. No wonder Jesus, in Matthew 23:33, called them "snakes." As we contemplate the meaning of grace, repentance (turning from sin), and the importance of forgiveness, we should remember this: The most harsh, critical words ever to come from Jesus were His judgments against the Pharisees. Jesus (the fish) was calling Pharisees (the snakes) devils. Why? Because they had not learned to give or receive grace.

# FISH: THE SIGN OF GRACE

Allow me to turn once more to the images of fish and grace portrayed so beautifully in the movie and book entitled *A River Runs Through It*. Its author, Norman Maclean, writes: "All good things—trout as well as eternal salvation—come by grace."

So I am not alone in seeing the fish as the sign of Christ and as a symbol of His grace—the free gift of love, salvation, and eternal life. This idea is not new. In the second century A.D., when the Roman Empire outlawed Christianity, believers connected the idea of a fish with Jesus. In order to avoid persecution, one of the secret codes they used to identify one another was a drawing of a fish. The letters of the ancient Greek word for fish, *ichthus* (Iota Chi Theta Upsilon Sigma), became an acrostic for the Greek phrase, "Jesus Christ, of God, the Son, the Savior."

So if two strangers met and were unsure if the other was a Christian, one would draw an arc like this: (. If the other man was a Christian, he would complete the symbol with a reverse arc, ), forming the outline of a fish ∝. A fish symbol drawn on a Roman doorway was a literal "sign of grace," indicating a safe house where other Christians lived or worshipped.

# THE CRUCIFIX FISH

God put an exclamation point on this symbol by creating the natural phenomenon of the crucifix fish (also called a "sailcat" fish). As a boy, I found the skeletal remains of a crucifix fish on the gulf shore. My dad explained this odd bone design to me. Clearly visible on one side is a cross with a figure upon it. The figure has two "eyes" and a crown of thorns, a hole at the point where his ribs might be (the wound in the side); and if you shake the fishbone, it has a rattle that sounds very much like dice being shaken and rolled (the Roman soldiers gambling for Christ's cloak). The back side of the fishbone looks similar to a Roman shield. The overall effect of viewing a crucifix fish skeleton is more powerful than any written description. It truly seems to be a message from God reminding us of Christ's passion upon the cross. Since Jesus had used the story of Jonah and the great fish to predict His death, the symbolism appears planned, not merely coincidental.

# GOD'S PLAN

The Crucifixion was a mysterious part of God's plan, a way by which God poured out grace upon us all—by the pouring out of Jesus' own blood. In the Old Testament, repeated blood sacrifices were used by the Hebrews to seek cleansing and atonement for sin. In Exodus 7:21, God turned the entire Nile River into blood: "The fish in the Nile died. . . . Blood was everywhere in Egypt." God did this to gain the deliverance of the Jews from slavery in Egypt. In the New Testament, however, only the blood of a single "fish,"—Jesus the Ichthus—was shed, cleansing anyone who will trust and accept His gift of grace.

The "fish as a means of grace" metaphor is found at still another place in the Scriptures. When Jesus was preaching to a crowd of thousands, lunchtime approached with no plans to feed the people. More correctly, the *disciples* had no plan, except to end the whole gathering and send people away early and empty. God had a plan all along. A kind little boy offered his lunch of bread and fish. The disciples, perhaps with a bit of arrogant humor, brought the meager lunch to Jesus in order to prove their earlier point: "This is all we have. Give up and send the people away." But Jesus gave them a lesson in humility, faith, and grace. He took the bread and fish, blessed it, broke it, and continued breaking off piece after piece until the entire crowd was miraculously fed.

On the eve of His death, Jesus solemnly broke bread with His disciples, preparing them for His upcoming sacrifice. He would be literally filleted (by whip and spear) and torn apart (by nails). On the cross, He became the broken fish who spiritually feeds the world. God's saving grace was and is sufficient for all people who come to Christ—that is, those who come not in the proud self-sufficiency of the Pharisees, but who come with the open and humble spirit of that little boy with his two fish.

And so, we have a clear choice: fish or snakes. Humility and grace or self-righteous legalism.

I'll have the fish, please.

TODAY'S PRAYER:

*O Lord and Savior, as You fed the five thousand with two broken fish, so feed us spiritually with Your broken body. Teach us the humility to receive Your grace and the promise of salvation. In the name of "Ichthus": Jesus Christ, of God, the Son, the Savior. Amen.*

# CHAPTER 5

# IN

# THE

# GARDEN

TODAY'S SCRIPTURES:

*Now the LORD God had planted a garden in the east,*

*in Eden; and there he put the man he had formed.*

GENESIS 2:8

*At the place where Jesus was crucified, there was a garden,*

*and in the garden a new tomb.*

JOHN 19:41

# THE GARDENER

The cool of the morning, just before dawn. It would have been a beautiful spring morning had it not been for the horrible images of crucifixion still imprinted on Mary's mind. And actually, it was still too dark to see the beauty of the flowers in the garden, the cemetery garden where Jesus' body had been placed three days prior. There was just enough light to see shapes, but not faces. Mary was startled to bump into someone and assumed it must be the gardener. Who else would be up so early among the tombs? Perhaps he was up early to beat the heat of midday sun, to till and plant, to pull weeds, to water, to bring life and beauty to this dismal spot of death. He was the gardener, but not the one hired by the wealthy landowners to tend their tombs. It was Jesus, the risen Lord—the Creator-Gardener who brought beauty out of ugliness, fruitfulness out of barrenness, health out of disease, and yes, even life out of death.

# THE PARADOX

I'm glad the Gospel writer included this curious detail about Mary mistaking Jesus for the gardener. Though easily overlooked, it presents in one small picture a striking paradox: a gardener among tombs. There in the place of the dead was a garden, teeming with life.

Jesus said that God the Father is a gardener (John 15:1), a vinedresser. God's act of creating humanity is portrayed in Genesis in terms of gardening. In the Garden of Eden account, Adam was made out of *adamah,* the Hebrew word for *ground* or dirt. Our entire blooming planet is testament to the fact that gardening—growing flowers and fruits, vegetables and trees—is one of God's favorite hobbies—and His favorite crayon is green (well, maybe second favorite. . .right after sky blue). Jesus, likewise, has an affinity for flora. He peppered His parables with agrarian images—sowers and seeds, orchards and fruit trees, pruning and grafting, farmers and gardeners.

# The Challenge

And it was in gardens that Jesus faced His greatest challenges. The first was a challenge of emotion and spirit, the second a challenge of the body.

When Jesus saw that His destiny was leading Him toward a painful death, He retreated to a garden called Gethsemane to contemplate and pray about the situation. He was "deeply distressed and troubled" (Mark 14:33–34) and said to His disciples, " 'My soul is overwhelmed with sorrow to the point of death.' " Christ's emotional struggle in the garden sounds even more intense than the physical pain He would soon suffer upon the cross—His second greatest challenge. My mental picture of the Crucifixion is of a barren, rocky, gloomy spot, but the Scripture states instead that, "at the place where Jesus was crucified, there was a garden" (John 19:41).

And that same paradox runs through all of life. We cry at weddings and tell jokes about death. Our greatest satisfactions and triumphs usually come after our toughest struggles, even after failures. In the same hospital on the same day, a grandparent dies and a grandbaby is born. The rose grows on the thorn.

# CONCLUSIONS

Two conclusions, polar opposites, can be drawn from this paradox. Some might say the thorns, the bad things in life, ruin the garden. I believe that the flowers bring beauty to the garden even if they have thorns. . .or adorn tombstones.

Being mature means that we are willing to accept life's pains alongside life's joys, life's darkness with its light, the greens mixed in with the grays. If we will learn from Jesus, we can make this paradox a practical help for living. As Jesus knew, whenever you are feeling overwhelmed, a garden can be a soothing retreat. Try to deal with the unpleasant things of life in the most pleasant environment you can find and with the loveliest of thoughts you can muster. Whenever you face hard decisions or experience dark anxieties, just remember that Jesus faced them, too. In the garden.

TODAY'S PRAYER:

*O God our Creator, we are grateful that we are never alone in the garden of life. We thank You for the beauty You have placed all around us. Help us to never lose sight of the good as we deal with life's struggles. Amen.*

CHAPTER 6:

# GOD AND THE QUIET HUNTER

TODAY'S SCRIPTURES:

*" 'But now I will send for many fishermen,' "*

*declares the LORD, " 'and they will catch them.*

*After that I will send for many hunters,*

*and they will hunt them down on every mountain*

*and hill and from the crevices of the rocks.' "*

JEREMIAH 16:16

The LORD said, "Go out and stand on the mountain
in the presence of the LORD, for the LORD is about to pass by."
Then a great and powerful wind tore the mountains apart
and shattered the rocks before the LORD,
but the LORD was not in the wind.
After the wind there was an earthquake,
but the LORD was not in the earthquake.
After the earthquake came a fire,
but the LORD was not in the fire.
And after the fire came a gentle whisper.
1 KINGS 19:11–12

# A Hunting Story

All hunters have tales of bravery and adventure from their time in the wilderness, stories that they are proud to tell their wives. But the best stories—the funny stories—are not always shared beyond the campfire. For example, I have a pastor friend who confessed the following incident. Let's call him Rick. Rick had enjoyed a morning of deer hunting one winter day. Loading up, he realized his hunting clothes were filthy, so he stripped off all his outerwear and tossed the soiled camouflage into the trunk. Dressed only in his underwear—okay, since he was alone in the deep woods—Rick closed the trunk and walked to the side door of the car to get his clean set of clothes. Finding the door locked, it suddenly dawned on Rick that after opening the trunk, he had reflexively put the car keys into his pocket—the pocket of his overalls, which were now locked in the trunk. So there he stood, nearly naked on a cold day, miles from anywhere. Even if help were nearby, he couldn't imagine walking up to some stranger's door in his Skivvies! So Pastor Rick did the only rational thing. He found the largest rock available and decided to break the side window of his automobile and retrieve his clean clothes. Fortunately, just as he was about to break the window, his son drove up and rescued him.

# Hunting Alone

Nonhunters may suggest that hunting alone as Rick did is foolish, even dangerous. But even when hunting in groups, most hunters eventually separate to their lone stands. Animals depend upon their keen sense of smell and hearing to detect predators, so chatty, noisy hunters will never see a deer. Gunshots aside, hunting is a quiet and solitary pursuit—which makes it a perfect setting for prayer and devotional meditation.

Spirituality has its social and loud aspects ("Make a joyful noise unto the Lord," the psalmist wrote), but hunting the heart of God can often be very much like hunting a hart in the forest. Picture a deer hunter alone in the woods at early morning, when most of the birds are quiet, the crickets have lost interest in chirping, the sounds of traffic and civilization are nonexistent, and all that the hunter hears is his own breathing. This is the sound of deep spirituality. The hunter can take advantage of this quiet to hear the still, small voice of God.

Civilization is fast and noisy. In most rooms of my house, if I listen closely, I can hear a clock ticking away, setting a pace and rhythm faster than people are intended to live by.

As the sun sets, crickets and frogs can make the wilderness noisier than my church study; but even then, it is a different kind of sound—more natural, more soothing, performed at a slower meter. The pulse of nature is not driven by the *tick-tock* and *clink-clank* of industry. Outdoors, we relax because we are removed from the tyranny of clocks and calendars and phone calls. We are not really closer to God, just less distracted.

# THE SOUND OF SILENCE

Meditate upon the fact that God is found best in that stillness. Consider the verse quoted earlier from First Kings: Elijah was running for his life and had spent the night, exhausted, in a mountain cave. After a long period of dire prayer, God brought reassurance to Elijah—but it came not in the mighty wind, earthquake, or fire. God's word of reassurance and redirection came in "a gentle whisper." Likewise, when Jesus wished to speak with the Father, He retreated from the noisy crowds into the distant hillsides or to still waters of the lake or into the dark hush of the night. Today, the harried urbanite will do well to follow Elijah and Jesus into the wilderness, and in those quiet places, learn the true beauty of this command: " 'Be still, and know that I am God' " (Psalm 46:10).

TODAY'S PRAYER:

*O Lord, God of Israel, enthroned between the cherubim, You alone are God over all the kingdoms of the earth. You have made the stars and the planets, and You can shake the very foundations of the cosmos. But You choose to speak to us in soft stillness. Help us find the quiet places where we can listen. Amen.*

## CHAPTER 7:

# GOD AS THE HUNTER (PART ONE)

### TODAY'S SCRIPTURES:

*I was senseless and ignorant; I was a brute beast before you.... You guide me with your counsel, and afterward you will take me into glory.... Earth has nothing I desire besides you.*

PSALM 73:22, 24, 25

*Job to God: "Bold as a lion you hunt me...."*

JOB 10:16 NRSV

## HUNTER AS PREY

If you are in the woods hunting deer (or turkey or dove or whatever), it might not increase your enjoyment to consider what being hunted—being the prey rather than the predator—is like. However, such thinking might make you a better hunter and make you a better Christian. Knowing your prey, thinking like the deer, may help you hunt them. Seeking the second part is more frightening. In biblical language, if God is the hunter, then we are the deer! God is hunting us. And what do most hunters do to their prey? They kill them.

# Pray You Are God's Prey

Does God plan to kill us? No. God does not hunt us in order to mount our heads as trophies on the wall. God hunts us because we are lost. God does not want to kill us, but He does wish to see us die—figuratively speaking. God wants to kill the worst in us so that the best in us can thrive. We are to die to self. Paul wrote, "You have taken off your old self with its practices and have put on the new self, which is being renewed in knowledge in the image of its Creator" (Colossians 3:9–10). Jesus said, " 'Whoever tries to keep his life will lose it, and whoever loses his life will preserve it' " (Luke 17:33). God wants to hunt and subdue the selfish animal in us so that the divine can triumph.

This presents a puzzle. If God wanted us to be purely spiritual creatures, why did He place us in fleshly animal bodies in the first place? Why was God not content with the angels?

# WHAT KIND OF CREATURES?

Maybe God wanted a creature who is more than a dis-embodied spirit. It is a mystery. The Bible states that God created humans "a little lower than the angels," yet "crowned him with glory and honor and put everything under his feet" (see Hebrews 2:7–8). "Lower than the angels" means we are placed in earthly, physical, animal bodies. Whatever kind of creatures angels may be, they do not have the same sensuality as humans. Despite our initial status as Angels, Second Class, we have the potential to grow beyond and above the angels, to take this miraculous combination of flesh and spirit, of terrestrial and celestial, and become some-thing even more wondrous than the heavenly hosts!

How do I know this? By reading the next few verses in Hebrews (2:8–10). The "him" in these verses refers to us—the human race. "In putting everything under him, God left nothing that is not subject to him. Yet at present we do not see everything subject to him. But we see Jesus, who was made a little lower than the angels, now crowned with glory and honor because he suffered death, so that by the grace of God he might taste death for everyone. In bringing many sons to glory, it was fitting that God, for whom and through whom everything exists, should make the author of their salvation perfect through suffering."

# DEAR DEER

Now, what has this got to do with deer hunting? Well, if we are the deer and God is the hunter, and the hunter is seeking to track down, subdue, and in some way kill our fallen "animal" selves, we can now see the purpose in it. God loves us dearly—pun intended. God allows us to strive for perfection through our physical existence. Even the pain of living in these frail bodies can be turned to the good. Christ took most of our suffering upon Himself on the cross. Still, part of the redeeming and perfecting process is something we must personally experience, suffer, and surrender. The death of selfishness is not without pain.

# ANIMAL FEAR

Somewhere in this process of becoming what God wants us to be, we shall face not only a figurative "spiritual death" of our sinful self but, finally, a real death of the body. The fear we feel about death is an animal fear, like the hunted prey who sees the arrow coming. But we are not animals. By faith, we must trust that something glorious waits for us, something transformational and transcendent. Again, Paul wrote that "our citizenship is in heaven. And we eagerly await a Savior from there, the Lord Jesus Christ, who, by the power that enables him to bring everything under his control, will transform our lowly bodies so that they will be like his glorious body" (Philippians 3:20–21). We will not just become some nebulous vapors, some ghostlike phantoms floating around in clouds. We will become, after death, all that is good in us now plus more than we can imagine.

C. S. Lewis gives us helpful images of this in his book about heaven and hell called *The Great Divorce*. In Lewis's fictional Heaven, the pilgrims who step into its outer boundaries find Heaven not some soft pillow of clouds, but a strong reality that calls for tough spiritual maturity—growth "into a Person"—a place where the watchword is "farther in and higher up" into "Deep Heaven." And Deep Heaven, while beautiful and glorious and filled with the Divine, is more "solid" and "real" than the earth we now walk.

# Set Free

Consider yet another verse from St. Paul: "The creation itself will be liberated from its bondage to decay and brought into the glorious freedom of the children of God" (Romans 8:21). Now we can better understand the metaphor of God as hunter and ourselves as the deer. God is not seeking to kill us and cook us over hot coals (as fire-and-brimstone preachers must surely do when they hunt deer!). God is more a hunter in the category of Marlin Perkins (of the old TV show, Mutual of Omaha's *Wild Kingdom*), who hunted down animals who had wandered from their natural and safe habitat and captured them only to set them free again in a better place, such as a wildlife preserve or animal sanctuary. God hunts us because God loves us. God hunts us because He does not want us to live as lost animals, but as perfect, content, spiritual beings in God's glorious game reserve, "Deep Heaven." And it is that very image of God that prompted the psalmist to write: "I was senseless and ignorant; I was a brute beast before you. . . .[But] you guide me with your counsel, and afterward you will take me into glory" (Psalm 73:22, 24).

Today's Prayer:

*O God, seek me, follow me, capture me with Your love, grab me up in the arms of grace, and take me into a glorious future. In Jesus' name. Amen.*

CHAPTER 8:

# GOD AS THE HUNTER (PART TWO)

TODAY'S SCRIPTURE:

*As the deer pants for streams of water,*

*so my soul pants for you, O God. My soul thirsts for God,*

*for the living God. When can I go and meet with God? . . .*

*Deep calls to deep in the roar of your waterfalls;*

*all your waves and breakers have swept over me.*

*By day the LORD directs his love, at night his song*

*is with me—a prayer to the God of my life.*

PSALM 42:1–2, 7–8

# THE HUNTER AND THE HUNTED

A long time ago, a young hunter hid among the rocks and trees with a crude weapon. He was not hunting for sport; he was hunting wild game for food, for his very survival. His name was David, a fugitive, running from a maddened King Saul, hiding in the wilderness, alone. We believe that many of the Psalms were written by David during that period of exile, when he was not only hunting for game but also was himself being hunted by King Saul.

Indeed, some of the Psalms could be entitled, "Prayers of the Hunter and the Hunted." For example, in Psalm 10:1–2, perhaps David was writing these words while on the lam: "Why, O LORD, do you stand far off? Why do you hide yourself in times of trouble? In his arrogance the wicked man hunts down the weak, who are caught in the schemes he devises." And in Psalm 31:1–4: "In you, O LORD, I have taken refuge; let me never be put to shame; deliver me in your righteousness. Turn your ear to me, come quickly to my rescue; be my rock of refuge, a strong fortress to save me. Since you are my rock and my fortress, for the sake of your name lead and guide me. Free me from the trap that is set for me, for you are my refuge."

Even as David felt like a trapped animal in need of refuge from hunter Saul, David also found comfort in remembering that he was also hunted, sought after, by God. In Psalm 139:5, David speaks of God as a hunter who has him trapped in divine love. "You hem me in—behind and before; you have laid your hand upon me." I'm not sure if many readers will carry this book with them up into their deer stand high in the forest canopy; but in those quiet moments alone in your hiding place, read or remember the Psalms of David and recall his trust in the Great Hunter. Use your imagination a bit to imagine how a frightened, solitary David felt utter dependence on God.

# The Hunter of Heaven

David sought God. But most folks run from the Lord or simply have no notion of where to look for Him. Lucky for us, God is reaching out to us, seeking us diligently. To twist Carson McCullers's poetic phrase, God is "the lonely hunter of the heart." God is, to use the words of Francis Thompson, the "hound of heaven." Some words from his famous poem may help you with your meditation on the topic of "God the Hunter":

*The Hound of Heaven*
by Francis Thompson (1859–1907)

I fled Him, down the nights and down the days;
    I fled Him, down the arches of the years;
I fled Him, down the labyrinthine ways
    Of my own mind; and in the mist of tears
I hid from Him, and under running laughter. . . .
    Still with unhurrying chase,
And unperturbèd pace,
    Deliberate speed, majestic instancy,
Came on the following Feet,
    And a Voice above their beat. . . .

The poem continues at length, its point being that the voice of the pursuing hound is God's. God hunts and tracks us until at last we realize, as Thompson put it toward the end of the poem, "I am He Whom thou seekest."

# We Still Flee

Sometimes, the thought of God as a hunter is not comforting but challenging, even frightening. We run. Sometimes we flee so hastily and blindly, we end up getting lost deeper in the wilderness. So we indeed do need God to hunt us down. We considered this at length in the previous chapter, but David had already, thousands of years ago, portrayed God as a hunter with bow and arrow in Psalm 38:1–2: "O LORD, do not rebuke me in your anger or discipline me in your wrath. For your arrows have pierced me, and your hand has come down upon me."

Yes, God is pursuing you vigorously, aggressively, like an armed hunter. God is not some wispy, vague force floating like a disembodied ghost about the universe. God is a real and personal being who created you, who longs to have you in His hand, who seeks you. But God also loves you and wishes you only the best, so you have nothing to fear. King David wrote repeatedly of God as "our refuge." Our safe place. So if God has hunted you down and caught you, rejoice, and go eagerly into that safe refuge.

TODAY'S PRAYER:

*O Creator and Pursuer, forgive us for our foolish flight. Bring us like lost sheep back from the wilderness into the safety of Your fold. Amen.*

CHAPTER 9:

# GOD AND THE BIRDS OF THE AIR

# BIRD WATCHER

Today I'm reclined at the same spot where years ago I found a crucifix fish—Gulf Shores, a beach resort not far from the mouth of Mobile Bay. Some fishermen are wading at the edge of the surf, casting; but I'm doing nothing but looking and listening, absorbed in the relentless crashing of waves against the beach and the loud cacophony of seagulls crying for food.

Seagulls are fascinating birds. If fish are God's miracle of the water, birds are the miracle of the sky. Motionless on the beach, a huddled mass of seagulls faces into the wind so their feathers are not ruffled. They are resting, waiting for some unknown signal at which they mount onto wings and fly. They don't seem to fly for pleasure. They fly for food.

Nowadays, the gulls survive mostly on bread crumbs and other scraps tossed by tourists; but if the gulls get hungry enough, they will go back to their old friend the sea and dive for fish. And then we see God's two miracles meet. Schools of shiners play near the water's surface. They gleam and refract the sunshine—and attract the seagulls. The birds dive quickly, without warning, and hit the water with frightening speed. Splash! They snatch the fish in their beak and, in an aerodynamic stunner, instantly reverse direction, popping back from the water and soaring again into the sky.

# KINGFISHER AND FISHER KING

In the Bible, just as a fish symbolizes Christ, a bird (the dove) is the symbol of the Holy Spirit who descended upon Jesus at His baptism, blessing Him. This same double imagery is found in two T. S. Eliot poems, "The Waste Land" and "The Four Quartets," in which Eliot hints of Christ as being both the "Fisher King" and the Kingfisher. The Kingfisher bird dives from heaven to earth. The "Fisher King" is a character out of the Holy Grail legend, none other than King Arthur, also a symbol of the resurrected Jesus. So when you see a kingfisher or seagull dive and catch a fish, you are witnessing multiple symbols of God the Father, God the Son, and God the Holy Spirit. I don't fully understand the complex symbolism of Eliot's poetry any more than I do the symbols of God found in nature. But take my word for it: Something holy is going on in both. I'm not suggesting that a hardened fisherman should start quoting T. S. Eliot to his buddies on the bass boat! I'm just making the case that I'm not the first one to see God's symbols at work in nature.

# LOOK AROUND AND
# SEE GOD'S SIGNS

Sometimes the cold and lifeless symbols in our church sanctuaries lose their power. We've seen the brass cross, the marble baptismal font, or the pictorial stained-glass windows so many times. Eventually, these objects fail to move us. So go outside with God in mind. Watching the gulls descending upon the fish reminds me not only of the Holy Spirit's descent at Christ's baptism but also evokes the Crucifixion and Resurrection. The Holy Spirit swept down from the heavens upon Jesus, the "fish" upon the cross, and snatched His physical life away. Three days later, the Spirit submerged again into the depths and darkness of death itself. By the Spirit's life-giving power, Jesus was snatched from Sheol—restored, resurrected. In a flash, the old world of life and death was changed.

I'm actually reminded of all that by sitting here on the sand, watching the birds dive and fish. If you think I'm crazy. . .well, perhaps you need a fresh encounter with the magic of creation.

# Magic and Mystery, Life and Death

When the God of heaven descended to earth, when the Spirit met the flesh (much as when the gulls swoop down to the fish), magic happened. Not the counterfeit magic tricks of charlatans and cardsharps, but the miracle-working "magic" of The Majestic. We fleshly creatures of earth and sea have been touched with eternity. We need reminding that we belong to the skies of the Spirit. And it is not merely "symbolic." We can be truly, supernaturally, changed. This godly magic is named by Christians as "redemption." It is the mysterious gift of immortality. St. Paul wrote, "Listen, I tell you a mystery: We will not all sleep, but we will all be changed—in a flash, in the twinkling of an eye. . .the dead will be raised. . .[and] the perishable must clothe itself with the imperishable, and the mortal with immortality" (1 Corinthians 15:51–53).

## Snatched from Death

Every now and then we get a glimpse, a preview, of what being snatched from death might be like. A friend of mine who lives on Fish River threw a party. Shortly into the festivities, a mother realized that her toddler had slipped away. They immediately feared the worst—that he might have headed for the riverbank. My friend ran to the water's edge but saw no sign of the child. Something told him to walk out onto the pier. He did so and peered through the clear waters to the sandy bottom. To his shock, he spied the little boy. He dived in with the speed and aim of a seagull and immediately retrieved the boy's limp body. No one knew how long he had spent on the bottom; but by all apparent signs, he was dead.

My friend did not surrender. He applied mouth-to-mouth resuscitation and extracted a good deal of water from the boy's lungs before he could begin to blow in air. Most of the small crowd that had gathered around them already had eyes filled with the tears of despair. After great effort, the child began to breathe, opened his eyes, and cried in panic. . . but he was very much alive! Now the tears of the crowd changed to tears of joy. They had seen death lose to life. They had witnessed a resurrection of sorts.

Today, if you have the privilege of attending the grand

showcase of water and sky, fish and birds, take time to contemplate the mysteries of flesh and spirit—and most of all, the miracle of immortality! When you see a bird dive into the waters and snatch a fish from the depths, remember that God has jumped into our world to snatch you from death.

TODAY'S PRAYER:

*O Holy Spirit, help us see heavenly glories reflected in earthly things. Descend to us, pour out Your miraculous life-giving power upon us, and lift our eyes toward the skies. Amen.*

# Chapter 10

# The Camouflage of God

Today's Scriptures:

*By faith we understand that the universe was formed
at God's command, so that what is seen was not
made out of what was visible.*

Hebrews 11:3

*"No eye has seen, no ear has heard, no mind has conceived. . . ."*

1 Corinthians 2:9

# Our Hidden God

It was the hardest question a pastor can field. And it came from a seventeen year old who was trying to sort out her life's direction and faith. "Why doesn't God show Himself to us?" I answered the young girl all too quickly. I should have shared with her that all of us wrestle with this enigma, as with the connected question "Why does God allow suffering?" But my answer was still genuine. God has shown Himself to us. . .and we killed Him! All that we need to know about God was revealed in Jesus of Nazareth, God in the flesh.

The second part of my answer is more nuanced. God chooses not to completely reveal Himself in all His glory and power. To do this would be so intimidating, we would cower in fear and be reduced to slaves or robots. God desires that we join the kingdom voluntarily, not out of coercion. To put this in terms of a hunting metaphor, God is camouflaged in order not to frighten away the deer.

Moreover, God doesn't want our mental picture of the Almighty to be limited to human, physical vision. God is too big for our tiny eyes. Maybe that's why God told Moses he would only be allowed to glimpse God's back in passing. The message of this book is that if you go outdoors and take a look around—an obvious example would be to stand on the edge of the Grand Canyon—you will get a better notion of the size and grandeur of our Creator than you would by viewing an 8" x 10" glossy photo of Jesus.

# We Add to the Camouflage

ʃadly, we must admit that we ourselves have veiled—camouflaged—the revelation of God in nature. . .mostly by paving over it! As the Joni Mitchell song puts it, we "paved paradise and put up a parking lot." I have a theory that atheists are born in cities, raised in small apartments with no view of the sky, and trapped in office cubicles where the only taste of nature is a smattering of potted plants (and half of them are plastic!). It's hard not to believe in God when one stands on the green and gray cliffs of Monterey as the ocean pounds the rocks, the fish swim, the birds fly, and you realize that your eyes and ears are wonderfully tuned to vibrate in sympathetic symphony to the majesty of it all. God is revealed in nature, especially in growing things, and eternity is reflected in the waters of the Pacific that stretch out as far as the eye can see. Wait a second—that's the point: The waters go beyond what the eye can see; we can't envision the whole thing. If the ocean is bigger than our vision, no surprise then that God is too big for our near-sightedness. We only see, as St. Paul said, in part, dimly.

A first-grader worked feverishly at her desk with crayons. The curious teacher asked what she was drawing, and the student replied, "A picture of God." The teacher said, "But, dear, no one knows what God looks like." To which the child replied, "They will when I get through!"

But of course, we don't. God is too huge, tremendous, glorious, omnipresent, and omnipotent. Our mind's canvas is too tiny to contain God, and our biases and prejudices distort our view. These principles are summed up in the great hymn by Reginald Heber: "Holy, holy, holy! Though the darkness hide thee, though the eye of sinful man thy glory may not see."

# WORMS, RAINDROPS, AND OCEANS

John Wesley said, "Bring me a worm that can comprehend a man, and then I will show you a man that can comprehend the triune God!" St. Augustine, one of the great bishops and theologians of the ancient church, walked along the beach by the sea, greatly perplexed about the doctrine of the Trinity. It was so hard to grasp, let alone explain, the idea that God is three persons in one. As Augustine struggled with this concept, he came upon a little boy with a seashell, running to the ocean, filling his shell, and then pouring it into a hole he had dug in the sand. "What are you doing, my little man?" asked Augustine. "Oh," replied the boy, "I am trying to put the ocean in this hole." Augustine learned his lesson. *That is what I am trying to do,* he thought. *Standing on the shores of time, I am trying to get into this little finite mind things that are infinite.*

Like a raindrop hitting the face of a mountain, when our tiny minds slam up against the eternal enigma of God, that very feeling of incomprehensibility is what should tell us that, indeed, God is God! If we could fully understand God, we would be gods ourselves.

So don't try to strip off God's camouflage. You don't need to see the fullness of God to have a full faith. Jacob wrestled an angel and caught a glimpse of God. . .and that was enough for him. Moses was only allowed to see God's backside. . .and that was enough. Samuel only heard the voice of God in the night. . .and that was enough. Blind Bartimaeus could not see Jesus at all yet had enough faith to be healed. And modern saints have continued that tradition: Helen Keller, blind and deaf, articulated a faith deeper, stronger, and better than any fully sighted person. Her faith was enough. Fanny Crosby, the blind songwriter, wrote, "Blessed assurance, Jesus is mine, oh what a foretaste of glory divine." Yes, she had enough "blind faith" to sing, "visions of rapture now burst on my sight." They all knew that seeing God was not the one thing needed. Faith is enough. But as Hebrews 11:1 reminds us, "Faith is being. . . certain of what we do not see." And for me, that is enough!

TODAY'S PRAYER:

*O Lord, give me the faith to "see" You with my soul's eyes. Whenever I view the vast expanse of Your oceans, remind me that You are even bigger than that. Amen.*

## CHAPTER 11:

# Something Dark in the Woods

TODAY'S SCRIPTURES:

*Be self-controlled and alert. Your enemy the devil prowls*
*around like a roaring lion looking for someone to devour.*

1 PETER 5:8


*The people walking in darkness have seen a great light;*
*on those living in the land of the shadow of death a light has dawned.*

ISAIAH 9:2

# Sounds from the Darkness

There was something dark and foreboding in the woods. . . . Well, actually, the woods themselves were dark and foreboding because the sun was just beginning to rise, the trees were tall, and the shadows long. My friend Danny had gotten an early start on his solitary turkey hunt and was already deep into the woods when it struck him how spooky the forest could be at that hour. He began to think about the vastness of the National Forest and the possibility of real dangers there—bears, snakes, bobcats, perhaps even a mountain lion. He wondered, would turkey shot stop a bear or wildcat? And then it happened. His fears became real. He heard the noise of another animal in the woods, and from the sound of it, a large animal. And it was coming closer.

# Real Danger

*S*omething very bad was indeed about to attack Danny. I'll leave you hanging for a moment about his predicament while I ask you to contemplate the matter. As beautiful and serene as the great outdoors can be, nature also has its share of dangers and evils. This is true of life in general. Life has joys and sorrows, opportunities and threats, good and evil. One minute we may be driving merrily down the highway with the stereo playing our favorite tune; and the next minute, a drunk driver may come over the hill in our lane. Life is fragile. There may be a fish bone destined for your throat. You may get an infected hangnail and die from routine complications. If you have too much life insurance, your "loving" wife may "accidentally" drop a hair dryer into your bathtub! Seriously, this life is always just a few heartbeats away from death.

As a minister, I have a close association with the Grim Reaper. I spend more time than I wish at hospital emergency rooms, funeral homes, and cemeteries. But if I may be allowed a statement that is, as Grandpa McCoy used to say, "no brag, just fact," when people in those situations look into my eyes, they do not see fear but faith. I don't know all the answers, I don't know all the mysteries of God, but I do know (as much as I can know anything infinite in this finite brain) that this life is not all there is. The miracle of life is not a temporary flicker of eighty-some years; God created us with eternity in mind. God has a plan for us beyond the place where the shadows fall in the forest. Up and beyond the dark valley, God will bring a sunrise over tomorrow's hill.

# THE SHADOW OF DEATH

My friend Danny came face-to-face with the shadow of death that day while hunting. He heard a noise and turned just in time to be hit in the face with gunfire. The "very bad" thing in the woods turned out to be that most dangerous creature of the forest: a human. A careless hunter had mistaken Danny for wild game. Luckily, it was turkey season, so Danny was hit in the face with birdshot, not a shotgun intended for deer. Shocked, Danny had no idea how severe his injuries were except that the faster his adrenaline ran, the more he bled. The good news: A hospital was not far away. The careless hunter had enough presence of mind to help Danny get prompt medical attention. He survived, though the shot had come close to blinding him.

# It's a Jungle Out There!

Most of us no longer face our greatest threats in shadowy mountain passages or in vine-tangled jungles. Cancer, heart disease, diabetes, and other ailments stalk us in our urban offices and rural factories. Moral dangers lurk around us, as well. Temptations to indulge in the pleasures of the flesh also bring dangers to the flesh (sexual promiscuity can lead to disease, drug and alcohol abuse can lead to addiction, etc.). The Bible describes the devil as a stalking lion. Nowadays, our adversary usually takes the form of other people: selfish or careless men and women who will exploit us, tempt us, cajole us, or drag us into the dark alleys of immoral behavior. It is not enough to be a passive Christian; we must actively be in communion with God's Word and presence for our souls to survive.

# A Light in the Darkness

Yes, there are dark and dangerous things out there in the jungle of life. And the greatest danger is damage to the spirit. If the darkness of our valley of shadows is internal, if our souls are empty and ashen, if we never seek the True Light, woe be to us. This spiritual truth is reflected in a physiological fact. Doctors have identified a type of clinical depression called "Seasonal Affective Disorder," appropriately abbreviated as SAD, caused by a lack of natural sunlight. SAD becomes more common in winter, with its shortened days, overcast skies, and our tendency to stay in the warm indoors. A simple cure for SAD is what this book recommends: Get outside on the sunny days and soak up the bright beauty of God's creation. The lift we feel under a cheery blue sky is not just psychological. Sunlight produces Vitamin D when it strikes human skin, and there are other beneficial chemical processes that fight depression, some involving the eyeball itself, all of which come by exposure to the sun.

Thankfully, God has sent life and light to us in His Son, Jesus, true Light for the soul and Life for the body. John the Beloved said it best: In Christ "was life, and the life was the light of all people. The light shines in the darkness, and the darkness did not overcome it" (John 1:4–5 NRSV).

TODAY'S PRAYER:

*O Lord, we confess our mixed feelings about darkness and light. Sometimes we like darkness—when we wish to hide. Sometimes we fear the light for what it might reveal in us. Sometimes we fear the darkness because we don't trust You to walk with us through it. Help us, Lord, to long for Your light, not only to guide us, but even to reveal to us the truth. Amen.*

CHAPTER 12:

# IN KING DAVID'S CAMP

# THE REAL THING

The most popular television show of all time was called "Campers." No, not really. But the highly rated "reality" TV series *Survivor* owes much of its appeal to the fact that people enjoy camping outdoors. A winner of the million-dollar prize on *Survivor* does not, it turns out, need to have great survival skills. On one show, nobody in the group could start a fire, so the TV host gave them matches; in another, when the "survivors" ran out of food, the TV host provided a cheeseburger. Winning was more about political and social skills. Nevertheless, that contrived outdoor drama has great appeal. In an age where real adventure is hard to come by, the idea of several ordinary folks going out into the wilderness with only the bare essentials to eat, sleep, and struggle against Mother Nature is exciting. Even if it's fake!

In our spoiled modern state, we will never return to the outdoor paradise of the Garden of Eden. The closest most of us can come to the real thing is to go camping. Camping can be used as a fun and invigorating spiritual retreat. Churches have long known this. Most denominations own large church camps, and children's summer camping programs are an important part of Christian education and spiritual develop-ment for our young people. Being immersed in nature is a big part of the experience; and, for some city children, it can be the first time they get a glimpse of just how awesome the Creator's handiwork is.

# Camping to Survive

In ancient Bible times, camping was not a sport or holiday. Camping back then truly was a story of "survivors." Camping usually accompanied two necessary tasks: hunting and making war. Hunters of old went on weeklong camping expeditions for the very survival of their village, not as a morning jaunt in search of trophy heads. Even that was much preferred to the war camp. Young men who went to war camp could easily become a "trophy head" themselves.

David's camp—more like a hideaway—would not have been much fun. It was a camp of loneliness, fear, and isolation. David was running for his life, hiding from crazy King Saul because he sought to kill the shepherd boy who had now become a warrior.

And yet, it was a good time in David's spiritual life because he *had* time. Time to think. Time to pray. Time to compose some of his famous psalms. Time to seek God's direction. Camping can do that for us. It gives us time to pause and meditate.

# It's About Time

Time. They say that good timing is the key to comedy. I think it is the key to most everything. If you invested heavily in the stock market on September 10, your timing was lousy. For football quarterbacks, for land speculators, for marriage proposals, timing is everything. In almost all things, if you take action too quickly or too slowly, you will fail. This is demonstrated by several contradictory—but equally true—aphorisms: "He who hesitates is lost," yet "Haste makes waste." Or, "Strike while the iron is hot," yet "Fools rush in where angels fear to tread." Are you able to recognize when the time is right?

Early in John's Gospel, Jesus announced that the time was "fulfilled," the time was right. Without giving them much notice, Jesus called the disciples; and immediately they left their nets and followed Him on what turned out to be a three-year camping trip. They knew the meaning of that Latin phrase *carpe diem*—seize the day, grab the moment. Jesus said to them, "The time is fulfilled," and they took Him literally.

The New Testament used two Greek words for "time"—*chronos* and *kairos*. *Chronos* is clock time, the daily tick that measures our minutes, and the root word for *chronometer*. *Kairos* means *the right time:* a special moment when everything comes together just right; a memorable experience that

112

strikes one in a powerful way; an instant of overwhelming insight from God. *Kairos* is *God's time,* the time when God is trying to tell you something special or fulfill His plan. Are you receptive to God's timing, God's *kairos?*

To receive a *kairos* moment, we must break loose from the clock-watching busyness of life and create space for God's time. We need to pace our lives so that the *kairos* occasions do not sneak past us unnoticed. Such moments can bring about confession, penitence, and growth.

## A Camper's Kairos

O ne such moment exposed my own selfishness. Years ago, I was camping out on a creek bank with a group of friends, including my brother. He had spread out a blanket on the sand for all of us to recline upon. Without thinking, I walked across the nice clean blanket to fetch something, tracking sand. When I returned, I subconsciously avoided the sandy spot that I myself had created in order to sit down on a clean spot. My brother pointed out my selfishness. "Lance, you tracked up the blanket, and now you expect someone else to sit in your dirt!" Well, I didn't do it intentionally. But as I stared at my sandy footprints on his blanket, I had a *kairos* moment. Those dirty footprints were a stark picture of my subconscious selfishness, my thoughtlessness. I was judged, not by my brother, but by my own footprints. That was one of many small but memorable events that led up to my return to Christlike living. It seems insignificant to you, perhaps, but I shall never forget it.

Have you had moments where you were caught in your own selfishness? It may not feel good at the time, but in retrospect I hope it made you a better person. . .and thus it was a blessing.

Such a moment came for King David. You know the story. He had committed adultery with Bathsheba, arranged for her husband to die in battle, and rationalized himself into complacency. . .until Nathan came along and confronted David with a story about a rich man with thousands of sheep who had stolen a poor man's only precious lamb. Outraged, David exclaimed, "The man who did this deserves to die!" Nathan looked David coolly in the eye and said, "You are the man." A *kairos* moment of judgment!

Thankfully, most *kairos* moments are blessed times of revelation or insight, where the truth or beauty of life breaks through to us in a powerful way. We've all had those meaningful moments watching a sunset or a child playing or singing songs by the campfire and felt a deep divine joy in God's creation.

One of my most moving *kairos* moments was not outdoors, but inside a hospital room. I lived for several years in an old house on the banks of Fish River. Living next door were distant elderly cousins whom I referred to as aunt and uncle. Uncle Louis was in his eighties. He had been a tremendous Christian and dear friend; but now he looked terrible, confined to a hospital bed, half of his body paralyzed by a stroke. His similarly infirmed wife, Aunt Mary, lived in a nearby nursing home, confined to a wheelchair. They had been married for over fifty years but now rarely saw each other. By sheer coincidence, one particular day I came to visit Uncle Louis on their wedding anniversary. As I talked to Louis, suddenly I saw his eyes light up. I turned around, and there came Aunt Mary being wheeled into the room. A relative had brought her to visit. She pushed Aunt Mary's wheelchair close to Louis's bed, and Mary reached out and held his hand. Frankly, they were a pathetic-looking pair, weathered by age and withered by disease; and Louis's face drooped on the left side due to nerve damage. But I have never seen anything more beautiful in my life. He looked into Mary's smiling face like a teenage boy admiring a high school sweetheart. All the years seemed to melt away. And he slowly said through his half-smile, "I knew you would come." For the first time in my life, I knew exactly what true love looked like. I felt it a holy privilege to witness such enduring love, a love that transcends age, wrinkles, infirmity, and sickness.

I had been there at just the right time. *Kairos*.

Are you receiving the *kairos* moments in your life? Are you making room for God to speak to you? Or are you stuck in *chronos* time, pointlessly ticking off the minutes, reeling in the years? Don't let life's best moments and messages pass by unnoticed. Now is the time!

TODAY'S PRAYER:

*Jesus, help me seize the day. Forgive me for the countless times when grace-filled, beautiful moments of splendor have slipped by me unnoticed. Open my eyes that I may see glimpses of truth You have for me. Amen.*

CHAPTER 13:

# IN JACOB'S CAMP

*He himself [Jacob] spent the night in the camp. . . .*

*So Jacob was left alone, and a man wrestled with him*

*till daybreak. When the man saw that he could not*

*overpower him, he touched the socket of Jacob's hip*

*so that his hip was wrenched as he wrestled. . . .*

GENESIS 32:21, 24–25

# WHINY CAMPERS

My father enjoyed camping and would have taken my brothers and me more often had we not been sources of constant whining. Don't judge us harshly. After a camp-out in the wet, tropical summer of south Alabama, we would need a blood transfusion because of the vampirism of swarming mosquitoes. I could have become a brilliant astrophysicist or genetic engineer if I had not inhaled so much bug repellent as a kid. See, I'm still whining to this day!

Since Scout leaders seem to have more patience with whiny kids than the average parent, many of my camping experiences came as a Boy Scout. During those memorable times in the woods, I learned a few things:

1. A warm, blazing fire goes out in a freezing rain.
2. You'll sleep much better on a mattress than in a sleeping bag on rocks.
3. A sleeping bag on dry rocks is better than one in a puddle of water.
4. Raccoons will eat *all* of your food if it is not sealed in a bank vault.

In other words, true, rugged, outdoor camping is mostly about discomfort and deprivation. Perhaps this explains why giant RVs and travel trailers sell so well. Nevertheless, even with all the negatives, camping—leaving civilization behind and diving headlong into the wilderness—can be a spiritual event, life-changing and rejuvenating. It was for Jacob.

# JACOB'S CAMP-OUT

Jacob's camp seems to be an extremely simple setup. He had a tent made of animal skin, maybe a blanket, and perhaps a robe folded up as his pillow. It was primitive and uncomfortable camping, but a Winnebago dealership had not yet moved to Jordan.

Jacob felt physically discomfited; but emotionally, he was downright tortured. His anxiety stemmed from the dread of an impending confrontation with his brother Esau—the same brother from whom Jacob had stolen his father's birthright and inheritance. He even feared that Esau would kill him when they met again. So Jacob sent lavish gifts and an apology ahead to greet his brother. Jacob's "repentance" may have been motivated by fear, nonetheless it was effective: Both Esau and God forgave Jacob and were reconciled to him.

The reconciliation with Esau was costly to Jacob. He gave Esau hundreds of his best livestock. The reconciliation with God also took a toll on Jacob. He wrestled with someone all night long, a man or an angel or God (Genesis implies all three), until in the end he received a blessing and God gave Jacob a new name, "Israel." After struggling with guilt over his mistreatment of Esau and even with a fear of death, Jacob's camping experience yielded a great blessing—

forgiveness and the beginning of a new nation. And there was a price to pay. Jacob's hip was damaged in the struggle so that for the rest of his life, he would walk with a limp—a painful and yet joyful reminder of his liberating encounter with an angel at the place he called "the camp of God" (Genesis 32:2).

My dad, Bob, should have been named "Jacob." He walked with a limp because of a damaged hip; and like Jacob, this was as much a blessing as it was an injury. Four of my uncles fought in World War II; and against the bloody odds, all of them came back alive. My dad was also drafted, but one thing saved him from the fatal statistics. He was declared "4F." That was the number for the form that certified a person as physically unfit for service. The doctor had ruled that Bob Moore's injured hip would prevent him from military marching and hiking. With 4F form in hand, Dad walked back through the lobby of the recruitment center, where some of his buddies still awaited their military exams. One of his friends joked, "Hey, Moore, you got your 4F, so you can quit limping now!" He didn't mind the good-natured kidding. He waited out the war safely on Grandpa Moore's farm.

# Hidden Blessing

The limp did not go away, nor did its blessing. The Moore family was poor and still recovering from the economic devastation of the Great Depression when Dad enrolled in seminary. His meager savings, plus working on the college farm, paid his tuition for the first semester. But as the second semester neared, Bob could find no source of funds to continue his education. He visited the dean in charge of financial aid, who found a small portion of tuition support for my dad, but it was not enough. Bob sadly told the dean that he would have to drop out of school for lack of funds. Head hung low, he exited the dean's office. But at the last moment, the dean looked up and called out, "Mr. Moore, wait a second. . . . Is that a permanent injury, that limp of yours?"

"Yes," my dad replied, "damaged from childhood."

"Well, then," the dean exclaimed, "we have a new scholarship available for the handicapped." And so, Bob became the first in his family to complete both college and seminary, thanks in part to the blessing of a limp.

I am Jacob's son, grateful to the wrestling angel. I firmly believe my dad was destined to be cannon fodder; but thanks to the intervention of Jacob's angel, my dad lived, and so do I.

Are there times when a pain or a struggle could later be

seen as a positive turning point in your life? Can you see now where a curse has turned out to be a blessing? Rather than running from guilt or problems, set up camp, wrestle with them face-to-face, confront the "dark night of the soul," and God will bless you come the morning.

## Today's Prayer:

*O God, keep us in the company of Your angels. Help us face adversity with faith that You have a plan for our lives. Give us Your blessing so that, in turn, we might become a blessing to others. Amen.*

# CHAPTER 14

# CAMPING
# WITH
# JESUS

TODAY'S SCRIPTURE:

*[Jesus] said to them, "Come with me by yourselves to*
*a quiet place and get some rest." So they went away*
*by themselves in a boat to a solitary place.*

MARK 6:31–32

# FACE TIME WITH THE SAVIOR

Wouldn't it be great to receive a personal invitation from Jesus to go away with Him "by yourselves to a quiet place and get some rest"? In Chapter 12, we mentioned that the twelve disciples were called to follow Jesus on a three-year camping trip. They went by foot, carried very few provisions, and usually slept under the stars. At times the conditions were unpleasant, though often they were able to find shelter in the home of a supporter. But the disciples did not know how fortunate they were to have three years of one-on-one time with Jesus—the rare privilege of camping out with the Christ, God in the flesh.

# CAMPING IS ALWAYS INTENSE!
## ("IN TENTS," GET IT?)

If you really want to get to know someone, share a tent with him or her. If your camp mate is a fine and loving person, you will enjoy the camp-out; and you will grow to love that person even more (assuming you are somewhat loving yourself!). If your camp mate is obnoxious, petty, and self-centered, you will find that out on a camping trip, as well. Spend some time "camping" with Jesus, and you'll learn more about the most loving person in the universe. Let me suggest two ways to actually do this while on a camping expedition.

# YOUR CAMPING ASSIGNMENT

The two pillars of personal spiritual discipline are prayer and Bible study. Bringing these with you into the camping environment can be powerful, offering a deeper dimension to your spiritual experience. First, try open-eyed praying. This means to speak with and listen to Jesus with our spiritual ears while our physical eyes feast on the cornucopia of God's creation. Psalm 19:1–2 urges us in this regard: "The heavens declare the glory of God; the skies proclaim the work of his hands. Day after day they pour forth speech; night after night they display knowledge" of God. Take a close-up look at the simple beauty of a grain of sand glinting in the sunshine, but don't try counting each grain on the creek bank. . . . Just revel in the fact that each one has been created by God to be as unique as a fingerprint. Or, while still praying, study the intricate tapestry of a veined maple leaf, which God has imbued with thousands of tiny cellular factories, each capable of converting a few rays of light into chemicals that eventually may become maple syrup! When night falls, put out your campfire, lay your head back, and gaze at the stars, constellations, and galaxies. Consider how vast is that black depth and how uncountable are its fiery orbs, and then realize how the mere fingertip of God can cover it all. As Job 12:10 puts it, "In his hand is the life of every creature and the breath of all mankind."

# A Guard Against Idolatry

Since ancient times and continuing to our current day, pagans have worshipped nature itself. Our purpose is not to make nature an idol, not to replace the Creator with a beautiful object of creation. By praying in the name of Christ and keeping our primary focus on God, we guard against this naturalistic heresy while still allowing God to speak to us through His handiwork.

Our second exercise, reading Scripture outdoors, also helps guard against becoming as the pagans who, as Paul warned, "exchanged the truth of God for a lie, and worshiped and served created things rather than the Creator" (Romans 1:25). If I stood atop the Rocky Mountains and gazed at their sheer size, I might understand why Native Americans worshipped the mountains themselves; but if I read Psalm 102, my worship is rightly returned to God. Verse 25 proclaims, "In the beginning you laid the foundations of the earth, and the heavens are the work of your hands." When I look closely at a flower and marvel at its complex symmetry and vivid color, I might read this passage from Isaiah 40:8, " 'The grass withers and the flowers fall, but the word of our God stands forever.' " I can revel in the rich beauty of a meadow filled with green grass and dotted with purple wildflowers, but all that glory is put in perspective when I read 1 Peter 1:24:

" 'All men are like grass, and all their glory is like the flowers of the field; the grass withers and the flowers fall. . . .' " Scripture alone has the power to truly humble us while proclaiming the majesty of God.

The Psalms are perfect reading for your "nature camping with Jesus" assignment, filled as they are with wilderness scenes. Even Scripture without allusion to the beauty of nature takes on new power when read outdoors. However, you will be surprised at how much of the Bible *is* set in the great outdoors, from the mountains, deserts, and valleys of the Old Testament to riverside baptisms and agrarian parables in the Gospels. One of the most important lessons from Jesus, the Sermon on the Mount, was delivered outdoors and is dappled with outdoor allusions, such as "the birds of the air," "the lilies of the field," fruit trees, rocks, and rainstorms. I offer this—Matthew 5, 6, and 7—as a perfect beginning for this experiment. Preferably, find a high mount and read "the Sermon on the Mount" aloud to your forest audience. (Okay, you think I'm nuts. But the famous Catholic priest Francis of Assisi regularly preached to the birds and the squirrels, and they made him a saint!) Even if you just read silently, you will never again view these Scriptures one-dimensionally.

So pack your Bible and your sleeping bag and go, literally, to camp with Jesus!

TODAY'S PRAYER:

*O Creator God, You reveal Yourself to us in nature. You reveal*

*Yourself even more fully in the incarnation of Jesus Christ. Help us to know You better by spending time with You in prayer and Bible study, both indoors and out. Amen.*

CHAPTER 15:

# COOKOUT
# WITH
# JESUS

TODAY'S SCRIPTURE:

*[When the disciples landed their boat on the shore*
*of the Lake of Galilee,] they saw a fire of burning coals*
*there with fish on it, and some bread. Jesus said to them,*
*"Bring some of the fish you have just caught. . . .*
*Come and have breakfast."*

JOHN 21:9–10, 12

# CHURCH MEAN/ EAT/

We modern churchgoers would have done well back in New Testament times—it seems they, like us, were always eating. We have church potluck suppers; and in a sense, the early disciples did too. Think of how many crucial events in the Gospels coincided with eating—the feeding of the five thousand, the argument between Mary and Martha before dinner, Zaccheus's life-changing meal with Jesus, the parable of the wedding banquet, the upper room Lord's Supper, the lakeside grilled breakfast with Jesus after His resurrection.

# SUPPER'S READY!

And no wonder. Aren't mealtimes the things we remember best? I remember so many special things happening at mealtime. I remember the sound of my mother yelling from the back porch to us kids, "Supper's ready!" I remember how special it seemed, too, to eat out in a restaurant. I can still taste my first oysters at Wintzell's Oyster House in Mobile, where the walls and ceiling are covered with humorous sayings and jokes. I remember family reunions. I remember good times with friends around a pizza and the first dinner date with my then wife-to-be. I remember the last Thanksgiving meal I had with my mother, because she died just a few days before our next Thanksgiving.

I remember the time in seminary when we were invited to the home of a Korean student. It was an odd meal. They had chopsticks yet were courteous to give us each a fork. . .but no knife! I wondered how we would eat the steak. My Korean friend, Mr. Kang, picked up his whole steak with the chopsticks and began gnawing on the bone like a chipmunk. I had to ask for a knife. They had no knives—that's right, not a knife in the house. So Mrs. Kang brought a pair of scissors and cut our steak into little pieces like a kid cutting out paper dolls. You can bet I'll never forget that meal!

# Remember

You've had meals you will remember all your life. But that is not what I want you to recall right now. Instead, think about the significance of Jesus' words at that Passover supper with His disciples, when He told them, "Do this in remembrance of Me." In effect He was saying, "Let the memories of this meal come back to you every time you share the bread and the wine of communion together. Remember."

They did not know the intense emotion this memory would later hold for them. In a matter of hours, Jesus was betrayed. Taken prisoner. Interrogated. Tortured. Nailed to a cross. His blood, poured out just as He had said it would be, when He poured the wine. His body, broken open by a spear, just as He had warned when He broke the bread. Imagine how the disciples felt when they went to their homes after the Crucifixion and sat down to eat a supper of bread and wine. Supper would never be the same again.

And Jesus told us, through parables, that the Passover supper was only a rehearsal for a meal yet to come—the grand and glorious banquet, the wedding feast for Christ and His Church, the day when we will sit down at the gate of the New Jerusalem to share a most amazing dinner.

# Fish and Grill

Jesus hinted at this in His postresurrection meal beside the Sea of Galilee. After Jesus had been crucified and His disciples were disheartened and confused, they did a wise thing—they went back to fishing. Anytime we face trauma in life, a smart therapeutic practice is to return to the most familiar and routine aspects of our lives as they were before the trauma, if that is possible. Or just go fishing. The disciples did both! While they were fishing, Jesus walked down quietly to the sandy shore and started a fire. After telling the apostles where to catch the most fish, Jesus returned to His role of servant. He carefully prepared a meal for them with His own hands—an outdoor, charcoal-grilled cookout. Then Jesus challenged Peter, "Do you love Me?" Then "Feed My sheep." And finally, "Follow Me!" When Jesus had first called Peter, He had said, "Follow Me," and it was a command, an induction into three years of service and hardship. Now, as Jesus spoke about death and afterlife and prepared Himself for ascension into heaven, the words "follow Me" were more of an invitation to life with Jesus beyond earthly death.

We are all invited to what the angels of heaven call "the wedding supper of the Lamb" (see Revelation 19:9). That true last supper isn't ready yet. But it's being prepared. Jesus set the table on that first Maundy Thursday, nearly two thousand years ago. He said then, "Drink of this, all of you." And in Revelation 3:20, John saw a vision of Christ proclaiming, " 'I stand at the door and knock. If anyone hears my voice and opens the door, I will come in and eat with him, and he with me.' "

When Jesus set the table on Passover eve, He was already, in His mind, setting the future table for you and me in the New Heaven that is to come. And He is knocking on your door, inviting you to that last/first supper in heaven—a cookout with Jesus. He's even preparing the food. I can almost hear my mother calling, "Supper's ready!"

## TODAY'S PRAYER:

*Our Father, You are our provider. You are the bread of life. We thank You for preparing a meal for us in heaven. May we never be so full of earthly food that we fail to hungrily anticipate that glorious wedding banquet in Your coming kingdom. In Jesus' name. Amen.*

# CHAPTER 16

# THE SPIRITUAL JOURNEY (PART ONE)

TODAY'S SCRIPTURE:

*I run in the path of your commands, for you have set*

*my heart free. Teach me, O LORD, to follow your decrees;*

*then I will keep them to the end. Give me understanding,*

*and I will keep your law and obey it with all my heart.*

*Direct me in the path of your commands,*

*for there I find delight.*

PSALM 119:32–35

# Hike to Nowhere

It was only a ten-mile hike. Even at thirteen years old, it should not have been a difficult journey for us. However, one of our Boy Scout leaders, intent on helping us get our merit badge perfunctorily and without distraction, chose to march us five miles alongside a straight highway and five miles back—in the peak of summer heat. The boredom was worse than the heat. The only pleasure in the whole journey was my canteen. With an eye only toward the goal of the merit badge, our leader had missed the deeper value of the journey itself. He took the short, easy, simple route alongside the paved road. I have since listened with envy as other Scouts have told about the joys of hiking on the Appalachian Trail, the delights of exploration and discovery on the mountaintop.

# The Journey Is the Joy

Far more tragic is when people span their entire lives using that same perfunctory method. Despite my strong belief in the importance of goal setting, I would argue that life is not a football game—crossing the goal line is not life's sole purpose. Learning, growing, sharing, and enjoying the travel are as important as the final arrival.

*The American Heritage Dictionary* defines a hike as "an extended walk for pleasure or exercise." Hiking is a journey with specific starting and ending points, for the purpose of enjoying the travel. My Scout leader had wrongly defined it as "the shortest distance between two points by which one can get a merit badge." He missed the scenic route. I hope he later learned that often the best parts of life are found on the detours.

When not distracted by glitzy trophies and looming goal lines, we may connect with our innate appreciation of the value of the journey itself. Many of our greatest fairy tales, epic poems, and novels are about *journeys*. Homer's *Odyssey* even uses the synonym for "journey" in its title. What is the most famous odyssey in history? I have two answers. In biblical history, it would be the journey of the Hebrews out of Egypt, through the wilderness, into the Promised Land. In modern pop culture, it would be the journey that Dorothy and Toto took along the Yellow Brick Road to Oz. Let's consider that first.

# The Yellow Brick Road

D orothy's hike along the Yellow Brick Road actually began on a dusty dirt road in front of her farm in Kansas. It was a journey of adolescence. When Dorothy's guardian, Auntie Em, failed at protecting her dog, Toto, the teenager struck out on her own. The purpose of her journey was not to reach Oz. In the end, Dorothy's only desire was to get back home, back to the very place from which she had run away. The person who asks, "Why take the journey at all if I simply end up where I started?" is like my tunnel-visioned Scout leader. Most people never catch the paradox of the Oz story because the tale is so well told; we become engrossed in the Yellow Brick Road journey, with its accompanying dis-covery, adventure, moral challenges, and the struggle against the forces of evil (a.k.a. the Wicked Witch of the West). Dorothy ended up back in Kansas, at the same old farmhouse with the same old aunt and uncle. Nothing there had changed. What had changed was Dorothy herself. She had achieved a measure of maturity. Through the joys and pains of her journey, she had become more confidently autono-mous, more her own person. As the good witch had said at the end of the movie, "You had to learn it for yourself."

In the original book by L. Frank Baum, another purpose for the journey is given. Dorothy had come to the end of her adventure and shared a parting conversation with the "Good Witch," Glinda. Glinda informed her that she could have avoided the journey entirely by using the power of her silver slippers (they were changed to ruby slippers in the movie). But then, the Scarecrow, Tin Man, and Lion all pointed out that each of them would never have received their gifts of brains, heart, and courage had it not been for Dorothy taking them along on her journey. So Dorothy agrees that the dangerous trip was worth it, saying, "I am glad I was of use to these good friends."

If I could speak my own eulogy, I'd like to say that about my life: "I am glad I was of use to my good friends." We must never believe that the end of life's journey, the goal of living, is just self-aggrandizement or personal pleasure.

# FROM SILVERY SLIPPERS
# TO GOLDEN CALVES

The exodus of the Israelites through the wilderness is another epic "journey" tale with many lessons to teach us—so much so that we will continue to discuss it in the next chapter. You probably know the story. The Jews were traveling from slavery to freedom, from the tyranny of Egypt to a place of autonomy in the Promised Land of Canaan. God miraculously helped them across the Red Sea and offered to lead them straightway into the Promised Land. But they grew impatient with the desert journey and allowed their eyes to wander from the holy prize to chintzy, glittering, golden idols. They showed all the human foibles that we, too, embrace all too often: lack of faith and trust in God; a tendency toward whining and negativity; unwillingness to follow good leadership; unbridled appetites and lusts; impulsiveness; and disobedience.

The consequence of their bad behavior and poor attitude was that they circled the desert for years, compounding their own self-created misery. It shouldn't take a genius to learn from the mistakes of their journey and apply it to our own. The virtues of love, trust, faith, positive thoughts, kindness, temperance, and moderation can change our journey in life from one of toil in the desert to rejoicing at the sight of the

Promised Land. The journey itself can be almost as good as the arrival.

With all this in mind, here is a helpful spiritual exercise you can try the next time you go hiking. Take along a pocket New Testament and read, slowly, the entire fifth chapter of Galatians. As you read, stop and consider how much better your life's journey will be if you truly try to incorporate the advice given there into your daily living.

TODAY'S PRAYER (ADAPTED FROM PSALM 119):

*O Lord, direct me in the path of Your commands, for there I find delight. Turn my heart toward Your statutes and not toward selfish gain. Turn my eyes away from worthless things; preserve my life according to Your Word. Help me journey in freedom as I seek Your precepts. Amen.*

CHAPTER 17:

# THE SPIRITUAL JOURNEY (PART TWO)

# LOST!

The most frightening, gut-wrenching feeling is to lose your sense of direction. Across the years, I have been lost in the woods, lost in a canoe, lost in my car, even lost on my bicycle. But the worst experience was when I became lost deep under a mountain in an unmarked cavern.

We began our journey with excitement and energy. Three friends and I planned to enter the lower entrance of the cavern, work our way through miles of passageways, and exit at the upper opening. This adventure proved again that having a clear-cut destination is not enough.

Three of us were experienced spelunkers; the fourth fellow had never been in a cave. This was a big mistake. Not because he held us back. . . To the contrary, the problem was that we "veterans" were so eager to show off our confidence, we chided the novice when, early in the underground journey, he stopped to draw an arrow on the wall pointing the way back to the entrance. "Don't bother," I explained. "We're not coming back this way. My cousin Dan, here, has been in the top part of this cave before. So all we have to do is keep going ahead and up until we get to the big opening to the upper level, where previous explorers have installed a rope. We use the rope to climb up, and then Dan knows the way out."

And indeed, we made our way with no problems and found the rope. Our novice friend was impressed with how easily and bravely we had found the way up. His respect for us instantly disappeared when we discovered that both the rope and the cave wall had become so wet and slimy that we could not ascend. It was like a climbing a greased flagpole. We had no choice but to reverse direction; and somewhere along the way back, we took a wrong turn. Hours went by. We grew tired and frustrated, but the real fear did not set in until Dan's light began to flicker. You have never seen true darkness until you have been in a cave with the lights turned off!

When Dan and I stopped to repair his light, he confessed to me in a whisper that he did not want the novice to hear, "Lance, I'm scared." That just about sent me into a panic, because *he* was the most experienced caver of all of us. I was counting on Dan to hold us together, to be the strong one. I murmured back, "I wish you hadn't told me that. . . . I'm frightened too." We were lost. We were wet and cold, and now we were on our second (and last) set of batteries. So we prayed. Not some casual prayer like I thoughtlessly give at mealtimes, and not some mostly-for-show prayer like we hear at the start of ball games. We prayed the real, heartfelt, sincere prayer of desperation—and trust. My panic subsided. All the sermons I had preached about trusting God in times of fear and trouble were validated. I had a real assurance that God was with us on our dark journey.

With renewed calm, we decided we would carefully backtrack and examine every possible turn and twist. After several dead ends, we finally found a familiar tunnel and knew we were headed in the right direction. But as fatigue began to overtake us, we came to a place with so many options and turns, for a time we went in circles. Claustrophobia! Then Dan announced, "Here it is." He had found the one arrow that our novice teammate had left when we had started. A lesson in humility had now been added to my learning about trusting God in the face of fear. In minutes, we escaped the underworld and stood shaken but euphoric in the sunshine.

## Losing Trust

Being lost on that journey through the shadows made me value God's light, direction, and faithfulness. God extended these same gifts to the Hebrews during their journey to the Promised Land. God had been faithful in freeing them from the Egyptians, leading them across the Red Sea, and leading them with a pillar of flaming light through the wilderness. Despite all that, they still lost faith and trust in God. . .and thus became, well, lost.

The Israelites managed to waste forty years lost in a relatively small desert, an area smaller than the state of New Jersey. They knew the sun set in the west, they knew the North Star, they were not geographic idiots. And, as mentioned, God guided them. But they grew weary and lost their vision and hope for the Promised Land. And for an extended period, they settled. They decided to give up on the journey, set up their tents in the desert, and just live there for years. Green fields and flowing streams were just a few miles away. But in their impatience and distrust, they settled. They quit moving. They gave up not only on the destination, but even on the journey.

This happens to modern folks, as well. Some are lost from the get-go; they never find God and never even begin the journey. Others discover that Jesus was right—the path to destruction is wide and easy, and they drift off the narrow way. And some, like the escaping Hebrews, settle for a modicum of comfort and never move forward toward the greater promise God has in store for them.

The spiritual journey of life winds, at times, through caves and dark valleys and through dry deserts and rough wilderness. But most of the time the journey itself is a joyful adventure, an opportunity to experience and learn and grow as we trust God to guide us to the Promised Land. Don't get lost, don't settle. . .journey on!

TODAY'S PRAYER (ADAPTED FROM ST. ALPHONSUS):

*O Jesus Christ, my Lord, with what great love You traveled the painful road of life. . .even unto death. And how often have I abandoned You. But now I love You with my whole soul. I am sincerely sorry for having offended You and for losing trust in You. My Jesus, pardon me, and permit me to accompany You on this journey. Amen.*

CHAPTER 18:

# THE CALM
# OF THE
# GREEN

# THE CALM OF GREENS

Hiking may not be the most popular pastime in America. And yet, there is a form of hiking that is becoming one of the fastest growing sports: golfing. Really bad golfers (like me) are basically just hikers with a titanium club instead of a walking stick! The appeal of retreating to the calming effects of God's green, growing outdoors is shared by golfers and hikers. So you hikers may pardon this slight detour in a section devoted to hiking and exploring.

Golf is holy (and no, I'm not going for the cheap pun on "holes"). The *American Heritage Dictionary* defines "holy" as "belonging to, derived from, or associated with a divine power; revered; living according to a strict system; solemnly undertaken; regarded or deserving special respect or reverence." All of that sounds like the ordered, methodical, contemplative sport of golf. Golf does for the soul something similar to religious meditation. It centers, focuses, and calms. One of the addictive pleasures of golf is how soothing the sport can be (especially when the ball rolls the right way). The somber, almost reverential, tones used by golf sportscasters hint that something more than competition happens amidst those eighteen holes. They whisper like nuns reciting rosaries in hushed tones at the altar.

This, along with Tiger Woods, explains why interest in

golf is booming. The busier and louder our workplaces, the more cramped our cities become, all the more attractive the sprawling greens appear. Even churches have gotten noisier with the increasing presence of loud sound systems, electric guitars, and drum sets. American society is craving the calm of the greens.

# THE GREEN PSALM

The Twenty-third Psalm continues to be the number one cited "favorite Bible verse," even though most people have never even seen a shepherd or a sheep. Most folks don't even have a green lawn. We long for the pastoral sentiments projected in that psalm: "He makes me lie down in green pastures, he leads me beside quiet waters, he restores my soul. . . . Your rod and your staff, they comfort me. . . . You anoint my head with oil; my cup overflows. Surely goodness and love will follow me all the days of my life. . ."

We yearn for still waters and green pastures; we ache to be soothed by God's calm goodness and loving grace.

## GRACE ON THE GREENS

Golf, like God, is full of calming grace. Even bad golfers can catch a break on a golf course. Yes, the most skillful putters usually win—but not always. Sometimes you just have a great day when the ball breaks your way, the hole magnetically pulls the ball in, and you feel, well, grace-full. Sometimes wind or gravity sides with the weak swing and luck leans to the undeserving. Grace. Maybe this is why such publicly sinful folks like Bill Clinton and O. J. Simpson love golf so much. They say Bill Clinton uses more mulligans, free drops, and foot wedges than one can count. I do not admire Clinton's ethics; but I find comfort in watching someone apparently more dependent upon grace, and so much more willing to accept easy forgiveness, than I. I am too self-reliant. I would be a better golfer if I would accept tutorials offered by the more talented. I would be a better Christian if I would be less self-righteous and more dependent upon God.

# Spiritual Exercise with a Golf Club

Let's face it. If you use a golf cart or a caddy, golf does not provide much aerobic exercise. But here are some spiritual exercises for golfers. Take a child or a nongolfer and teach him or her the game. This will be an exercise in patience. If you are saintly, you will also purposely play poor. It builds humility and relationships. Another exercise is the opposite: Ask the very best golfer you know to play a round with you, "so that I can learn from the master." The final spiritual exercise I offer you is only for nine holes. Allow yourself the same amount of time you might usually budget for the full course, and now, for just nine holes, focus only on relaxing. Focus not on your swing, not on winning, not even on playing well, but on relaxing. Breathe deep, stay calm, and laugh at yourself when you slice into the woods. Go solo—no partners, no caddies, no cart. Repeat the Twenty-third Psalm once for each hole. Listen to the birds and their carefree singing, watch the squirrels as they play their games of chattering chase, and remember that "sport" and "play" were inventions of God. And be grateful. Take in the manicured beauty of the greens, soak up the sun, and drink with your soul the blueness of the sky; and thank God for the gift of that thing we now call "a day off," formerly called "the Sabbath." Okay, wait a second. . . I'm not saying to do this on a Sunday during the worship hour! I'm merely reminding you that God, in His wonderful, wise, and loving plan for humanity, designed a weekly day of rest. Hopefully, you can get a Saturday and a Sunday off, and you will divide this time unselfishly among your church, your family, your relaxing home activities, and a bit of calm time on the green with God.

## TODAY'S PRAYER:

*O Good Shepherd, teach me patience and humility. Lead me away from the hustle and bustle into the calm center of Your grace. Bless me with such an abundance of grace and mercy that it overflows to those around me. In Christ's name. Amen.*

CHAPTER 19:

# IN THE VALLEY OF SHADOWS

TODAY'S SCRIPTURES:

*Yea, though I walk through the valley of the shadow*

*of death, I will fear no evil: for thou art with me;*

*thy rod and thy staff they comfort me. . . .*

*Surely goodness and mercy shall follow me*

*all the days of my life: and I will dwell*

*in the house of the LORD for ever.*

PSALM 23:4, 6 KJV

*What has happened to me has really served to advance the gospel. As a result, it has become clear throughout the whole palace guard and to everyone else that I am in chains for Christ. Because of my chains, most of the brothers in the Lord have been encouraged to speak the word of God more courageously and fearlessly.*

PHILIPPIANS 1:12–14

# CRI/I/ CREATE/ CHARACTER

M any people have said something to the effect of, "I found God in the darkest valleys of my life." Me too. The message of this book has been that God is found everywhere, especially out in the beauty of nature. Nearly three thousand years ago, the psalmist saw that God could be found both in the darkest valleys and in the beautiful green meadows. Perhaps while reclined on a grassy hillside looking down into the shadows of the valley, David wrote that the Lord is like a shepherd who walks with his sheep through the shaded places where predators crouch. And ever since, many of us have found that in the face of darkness and even death, we sense God's presence more vividly.

We also know that good often comes to us out of life's adversities. In the 1960s, a psychologist named Robert Coles completed an in-depth scientific study on stress. His data showed that stress and conflict greatly increase one's growth and personal development. We didn't really need science to tell us what life has already taught. Crisis creates character.

Knowing this, however, does not make us welcome trouble nor does it free us from a fear of life's shadows. Crisis may build character, but impending trouble can breed fear. And fear can be destructive. Usually our nightmares and worries about life are worse than the problems themselves. We are all too much like the patient diagnosed with ulcers. After the doctor explained that often ulcers are the result of worry, he asked, "What have you been so anxious about?" The patient replied, "I kept worrying I'd get an ulcer." It is often not the actual crisis that hurts us; instead, what really intimidate us are the towering imaginary monsters that fear has created in our own minds.

The Shepherd Psalm is a good antidote for that fear. When faced with trouble, we should repeat to ourselves, "Though things look dark, I shall not fear, for God is with me." The Shepherd's Habit is an even greater antidote.

# THE SHEPHERD'S HABIT

David practiced turning his fear over to God by looking to God's presence in the outdoors. When Goliath threatened to make mincemeat of the young shepherd boy, David thought back to times in the wilderness when God had been with him to successfully battle the lion and the bear. When King Saul chased David with a spear, he retreated to the hills. As he contemplated the vast power and beauty of God evidenced in creation, David found comfort and refuge. We can do something similar. When your boss yells at you, go sit by a tumbling brook and listen to the soothing sounds of the water. You might hear God's voice in it. When disagreements with your family or friends loom large, stand on a mountain and take a good look at something much bigger than your problems. When you lose a loved one to death, go out and gaze at the stars. . . . It may be the closest you can come to seeing eternal life. When your creditors call and you wonder how you will pay your overdue bills, look at the birds in the trees outside and hear the words of Jesus: " 'Do not worry about your life, what you will eat or drink; or about your body, what you will wear. . . . Look at the birds of the air; they do not sow or reap or store away in barns, and yet your heavenly Father feeds them. Are you not much more valuable than they?' " (Matthew 6:25–26). The great outdoors holds great power over problems.

# THE PRISONER'S PLAN

St. Paul also gives us guidance through our dark valleys. Paul suggested to the Philippians that they actually had control over crises. No, we don't control everything that happens to us. But we can control far more than we admit. We are too quick to blame bad luck for our own failures. Even when we are innocent victims of calamity, Paul argues that we can still fully control our response to crisis. And he should know. Paul, chained in prison, alone, cold, and hungry, proclaimed: "What has happened to me has really served to advance the gospel" (Philippians 1:12), and "I have learned the secret of being content in any and every situation" (Philippians 4:12). Paul also boasted in his letter to the Philippians that his imprisonment had afforded him a new ministry—to prisoners and guards. The Living Bible renders his words this way: "Because of my imprisonment many of the Christians here seem to have lost their fear of chains!" (Philippians 1:14). What a difference one's point of view makes! Paul saw his crisis as an opportunity and, in so doing, freed others of their fears.

When we say the word "crisis," we usually think of catastrophe, calamity, something awful. That's not really what the word means. The dictionary defines it as a turning point for good or bad. In the original Greek, the word "crisis" came from the word for decision or judgment. In Chinese, the symbols for *crisis* (wei ji) are also used as the symbols for *opportunity*.

So a crisis is, literally, an opportunity for positive change. We can choose to face adversity with either hope or despair, just as we can walk the valley of shadows with or without God.

Actually, you can't choose to walk without God; God will be there in the valley whether you recognize Him or not, whether you follow God's guidance or stumble blindly down your own path.

The Christian life does not remove the darkness, but it does offer a light *in* the darkness, a presence and power in the midst of the valley of evil. Look again at how David words it: *"Even though* I walk through the valley of the shadow of death, I will fear no evil, for you are with me" (emphasis mine). For me, that's enough.

TODAY'S PRAYER (BASED ON PHILIPPIANS 1:18–19):

*Gracious Shepherd, even though I walk through dark valleys in my life, I will continue to rejoice in You, for I am confident of this one thing: That through Your help, all that happens to me will turn out for my deliverance. In Christ's name. Amen.*

CHAPTER 20:

# ON THE
# MOUNTAINTOP

TODAY'S SCRIPTURES:

*Great is the LORD, and most worthy of praise,*

*in the city of our God, his holy mountain.*

*It is beautiful in its loftiness, the joy of the whole earth.*

PSALM 48:1

*After six days Jesus took Peter, James and John with him*

*and led them up a high mountain, where they were*

*all alone. There he was transfigured before them.*

MARK 9:2

# Getting There

We were headed to the mountains, but first we had to cross the desert. My friend Billy and I were driving through the endless desolation of West Texas and Arizona, headed toward the Colorado mountains. We were in our early twenties with very little money and an old Dodge Dart, which began to overheat in the hundred-degree heat. With no water in sight, I reluctantly suggested a solution: I had read that in an emergency, one can expand the cooling capacity of a radiator by turning on the car heater. It worked. The engine temperature lowered enough for us to keep driving. Now the only things overheating were the passengers. No water, the sun bearing down, the outside temperature above one hundred, and there we were driving along with the heat on! We laughed at the absurdity of our predicament. And we survived.

# TOP OF THE WORLD

Within twenty-four hours, we had made it up the southern Rockies to a snow-covered campsite by a beautiful mountain lake. The contrast was striking: We had gone from hot, arid flatland to a cool, wet, green mountainside in a matter of hours. As I stood there on a high cliff and gazed out across the gorgeous planet, I felt God's presence in a powerful way. Having gone through the "hell" of the desert, no wonder the mountain felt like heaven! And I could almost hear God speaking to me through my emotional exhilaration, saying, "This is a holy place." I also heard the inner voice of God saying, "If I can make all this expansive splendor, why can't you trust me more with your small life?"

And I thought of how many times in the Bible the prophets and apostles climbed to the top of mountains to seek a word from God. Noah built an altar to God on Mount Ararat. Abraham encountered God on a mountain called "God Will Provide." Moses received the Ten Commandments on Mount Sinai. Elijah climbed Mount Carmel to call upon the Lord. Jesus brought His disciples to a mountaintop to witness His supernatural transfiguration.

# MOUNTAINTOP EXPERIENCE

All this helps explain why, in popular Christian jargon, a "mountaintop experience" refers to a highly emotional spiritual conversion or epiphany. One of my earliest mountaintop experiences occurred at sea level, at summer camp as a child. The "high" (another mountain-related metaphor!), which came from connecting with God at an emotional level, lasted about three days. Then my camp friends and I returned to our usual lackluster interest in Jesus and church. That's usually the way it goes. Dramatic conversions, tear-filled confessions at an altar, and emotional revelations of God are singular events that alone cannot sustain a Christian's commitment for a lifetime. This doesn't invalidate what I experienced. Our emotions are an important part of what makes us human. Feelings have value, and a part of our spirituality is connected to sentiment—connected but not synonymous. We must never substitute emotion for real spirituality. God relates to us through our feelings, but also through our minds, our bodies, our wills. This is why Jesus commanded us to " 'Love the Lord your God with all your heart and with all your soul and with all your mind and with all your strength' " (Mark 12:30). Jesus also commanded us to worship God "in Spirit and in Truth." Our worship and spirituality should be holistic, involving our God-given brains as well as our emotions. Anything less than worshipping God with our whole being can put us on a slippery slope that descends to idolatry.

# FALLING OFF THE MOUNTAIN

Speaking of slippery slopes, when Billy and I made our way down the mountain in his trusty, rusty Dodge Dart, the snow turned to rain and the road turned to slippery mud. And there were no guardrails. At one curve in the primitive road, Billy lost control of the steering and the braking. The mud was so slick, the car began slowly sliding straight ahead toward the edge of the cliff. Unbelievable as it may sound, we actually jumped out of the car and began to push against it. Our feet were better at digging into the soft mud than were the bald tires, and so we managed to stop the car at the last moment.

There is a grave danger on the spiritual mountaintop, too. In my emotional exuberance, I may overlook the need to love God with my mind and soul. Reason and will are our God-given protective guardrails that keep us from falling off the mountain. The Bible even warns of the danger of an actual mountaintop event. When Jesus was directly tempted by the devil, this is what happened:

> *Again, the devil took him to a very high*
> *mountain and showed him all the kingdoms of the*
> *world and their splendor. "All this I will give you,"*
> *he said, "if you will bow down and worship me."*

*Jesus said to him, "Away from me, Satan! For it is written: 'Worship the Lord your God, and serve him only.'"* (Matthew 4:8–10)

The worship of power and money could tempt anyone away from worship of God, but a temptation that often ensnares Christians is the mountaintop experience. I have seen Christians seek the easy rush, the passionate high of religious experience, instead of the hard, daily path of loving service to God. Contemporary Christianity spends much time, money, and effort on exciting rallies, concerts, big-name revivals and retreats, which have some value. But if a Christian hops from one event to another, spending all his or her free time and disposable income on these grand festivals of religious highs, how much is left for service down in the valley? True worship of God isn't just on the mountaintop. True worship isn't just a warm fuzzy in the heart. True worship means putting ourselves fully into Christian servanthood. As Romans 12:1 puts it, "Offer your bodies as living sacrifices, holy and pleasing to God—this is your spiritual act of worship."

# Transfigured. . .Now What?

After you've had an emotional, mountaintop religious experience, the next step is to ask: "What do I do now?" Jesus took Peter, James, and John with Him up a high mountain where He was transfigured before them. We don't exactly know what to make of that. The dictionary defines transfiguration, in part, as "a transformation that glorifies or exalts." In a bright white light, Jesus was seen with the spirits of Moses and Elijah and heard the affirming voice of God. The disciples had no idea how to respond. Flummoxed and amazed, all that Peter could manage to say was some nonsense like, "Let's build three booths, three shrines to commemorate this." But Jesus instructed them to do otherwise. The voice of God on the mountain had declared to them: "This is My Son, whom I love; with Him I am well pleased. Listen to Him!" And this is exactly what our response to a moving religious "high" should be. We should go back down to level ground and listen to Jesus. Reading the Bible, especially the words of Jesus, is what can sustain our religious fervor and our long-term, mature commitment to God.

The next step is, as already mentioned, to serve others. The very next thing Jesus did after the transfiguration was to heal a sick boy.

I do not discourage you from making an occasional pilgrimage to the mountaintop, both physically and spiritually. We need to get our spiritual batteries recharged; and certainly, a dry intellectual religion barren of excitement, emotion, and energy is no better than a religion based only on feelings. Sometimes we just need to get out of our cubicles, climb the highest mountain, and take an awe-inspiring breathless look at the vast world unfolding in quiet glory at our feet.

Just be careful going down.

TODAY'S PRAYER:

*O Lord, thank You for the precious times when You have touched me at the point of my emotional need. Help me to balance head, heart, will, and feelings, that I might put my whole self into Christian worship and service. Amen.*

CHAPTER 21:

# GRANDPA MIK'S SHRIMP BOAT

# MORE THAN I COULD COUNT

Fishing with my father was one of the more memorable experiences of my childhood. Having come from a generation in which men seldom expressed love for their sons in words, one of the ways my father expressed his love for us was by taking us fishing. During those long, quiet hours on the water, Dad would teach us theology in a casual, nonlecturing style that we enjoyed more than his Sunday sermons. Ironically, the one thing he failed to teach us was how to become good fishermen! We just didn't have much success. He blamed it on our impatience and noisy movements in the boat. But I had concluded that there just were not many fish in the water. I calculated about one small fish for every million gallons! Soon I learned how small my thinking had been.

An older friend of my father's invited our family to go out on his shrimp boat for an afternoon. Most of us called him Grandpa Mik, even though he was not any blood kin to me. He greeted me with a smile and these words, "Do you think that iron can float?" And at eight years old, all I knew to say was, "No." Then he laughed and said, "Well, I hope you don't mind coming on board, because the hull of this boat is made out of iron." Iron can indeed float.

On his shrimp boat, I learned that the waters were teeming with fish. I also learned that a net is a far more efficient way to catch fish than a rod and reel. And Grandpa Mik's shrimp net caught them in greater variety. He caught speckled trout, flounder, puffer fish, croakers, crabs, saltwater catfish, baby sharks, and other odd fish we couldn't even identify. And yes, shrimp. When he would winch the large net aboard and dump its wriggling, flopping contents onto the wide back deck, it thrilled me. Fish jumping everywhere, crabs crawling away, a countless multitude of shapes and colors, all pulled magically from the sea.

# DON'T THINK SMALL

Whenever I remember my expedition on Mr. Mikkelsen's shrimp boat, the parable of the net from Matthew 13 comes to mind. Jesus was trying to explain, yet again, the way the kingdom of God works. We tend to think of God's kingdom in small and individualistic terms. When we read about being a "fisher of men," do we not get a mental image of a lone fisherman with a cane pole? That isn't how Jesus envisioned it. He described a net, not a rod and reel. The net brought in "all kinds of fish." The audience listening to Jesus believed that the kingdom would be limited to their "chosen race," the few, the "elect." Jesus knew that God's net is cast far and wide and commanded them to "go and make disciples of all nations." Some of the Jews had a very narrow view of humanity. In the minds of the overly proud Pharisees, Gentiles were unclean, almost subhuman. They could not imagine being lumped together with all the riffraff in the same net of God. But Jesus taught a radical notion of universal invitation and inclusion.

# Throwing Some Back

However, in that same parable, Jesus taught a hard word: The wicked will be separated from the righteous. On Grandpa Mik's shrimp boat, as soon as the net was emptied on board, it was our job to pick out the good fish from the bad. Some fish were not tasty. Some were too small or too bony. And some were not fish at all. The eels, the baby sharks, the seaweed, and even the occasional boot or tire—these were all thrown back into the ocean. Jesus warned that a similar sorting would take place before we are allowed into God's kingdom.

Most of us are not troubled with the idea of truly evil people being tossed out of the net, forbidden to enter the kingdom. If Joseph Stalin, Adolf Hitler, and Saddam Hussein were allowed to inhabit and terrorize heaven, it would not be heaven at all. They would transform Paradise into Hades. God upholds the principle of justice while balancing it against grace.

But what of those aboriginal tribes who honestly sought God but never knew Christ, or those who died as very young rebels and never had the opportunity to grow into a love of God? Does God extend grace to them? We should not presume to answer these mysteries. But we can trust that God is both just and loving; and even in the parable of the net, we may find the possibility of hope for some of the lost. You see, some of those fish that were too small to keep, having been thrown back into the ocean, would eventually grow bigger, be caught up in the net another time, and kept. Jesus had observed this many times as He watched the Galilean fishermen. Even when Jesus mentions, in the same passage in Matthew, that the wicked will be thrown in the fiery furnace, we still find the possibility of grace. Of the many references in the Bible to furnaces and fires, far less than half refer to a destructive flame; most of these refer to a refiner's fire, a process for burning away the impurities, the dross, to reveal the pure gold and silver.

And there is one other lesson I learned from my trip on Grandpa Mik's shrimp boat: God's plan is bigger than the vast ocean, deeper and more mysterious than its depths. Never underestimate God. You see, twenty years later, Mr. Mikkelsen's granddaughter was the best catch I ever made. She became my wife, Diana.

Today's Prayer:

*O Lord, help me trust in Your eternal plan. Catch me up in Your kingdom net. Do not discard me. And guide me to work with others You have captured by Your love to be successful "fishers of men." In Christ's name. Amen.*

# Chapter 22

# Boating Buddies

**Today's Scriptures:**

*And Jonathan made a covenant with David because
he loved him as himself. Jonathan took off the robe
he was wearing and gave it to David, along with his tunic,
and even his sword, his bow and his belt.*

1 Samuel 18:3–4

*Two are better than one, because they have a good return
for their work: If one falls down, his friend can help him up.
But pity the man who falls and has no one to help him up!*

Ecclesiastes 4:9–10

# A Boat Built for Two

Robert Fulghum wrote a classic entitled *All I Really Need to Know I Learned in Kindergarten*, filled with sage advice for adult living based on the lessons we should learn as toddlers. One of the jewels he offers is to "find a buddy and hold hands when we cross the street"—reminding us, of course, about the great value of friendship. Only fools and spiders go through life alone. One reason that sporting is such a popular undertaking for men is that it gives us an excuse to be together as friends. Most of the sports described in this book can be done solo, yet they rarely are.

For example, I am a passionate boater with a passionate rule: Never boat alone. Most deaths and injuries on the water involve one of two things—beer or solitude. A drinking buddy on a boat is a recipe for trouble, but so is being sober and solo. Fall out of a boat with the motor running (which happens surprisingly often), and you'll wish you had a buddy in the boat!

This is a biblical principle: "Though one may be overpowered, two can defend themselves. A cord of three strands is not quickly broken" (Ecclesiastes 4:12). We would do well to honor it. Having friends who golf, fish, and hunt with you is one of the keys to a full life and even to spiritual growth.

The Bible begins with this lesson. When the first human was created, God said, " 'It is not good for the man to be alone' " (Genesis 2:18). The vast majority of Bible heroes were not loners. Besides the support of good wives, most of the men of the Bible had "golfing buddies": Moses had Aaron, David had Jonathan, Job had Bildad (well, maybe not the most supportive friend in the world!), Elijah had Elisha. Jesus, in addition to His disciples, had His friend Lazarus; and Paul had Barnabas. And with the women, Naomi had Ruth, and Mary had Martha. We could cite many more examples.

# THE TRUTH ABOUT RUTH

A moving account of biblical friendship is the story of Ruth and Naomi. Naomi's husband had died, and financial hardship forced her to pack up and move back to her homeland. Her daughter-in-law Ruth made her famous statement of faithful friendship, immortalized in the wedding song, "Whither Thou Goest, I Will Go." So Naomi did not have to travel alone. Ruth's friendship for Naomi brought Ruth to a new land, where she met and married a good man named Boaz; and they all lived happily ever after. The interesting thing about the story is that from the marriage of Ruth and Boaz came the lineage of the House of David, and thus the birth of Jesus of Nazareth. The Messiah was literally the product of a devoted friendship hundreds of years before Jesus' birth! Jesus reciprocated. He said in John 15:15, " 'I no longer call you servants. . . . I have called you friends.' "

Dr. Leonard Sweet reports the measurable value of friendships in his book *The Jesus Prescription for a Healthy Life*. "Friends can save your life, literally," he writes. "Tests and reports from around the world now demonstrate that warm social ties and secure relationships can boost immune functions, improve the quality of life, and lower the risk of dying from cancer, coronary heart disease, and other physical and mental health conditions. . .and decrease. . .susceptibility to illness by participating in small groups."[2]

He goes on to say that men, in particular, are lacking in intimate friendships and that this might explain why women outlive us.

# NO SOLO

If social isolation harms us physically, it probably harms us spiritually, too. Jesus, Moses, Daniel, and other spiritual giants would regularly retreat for private prayer, meditation, and devotional time with God; and in this very book, I recommend you do the same. However, no one in the Bible is portrayed as a spiritual Lone Ranger. Time alone with God was always meant to improve the time later spent in the company of friends. When John wrote the Book of Revelation, he was in exile on the island of Patmos. We picture him as a hermit. But what was he doing? He was writing letters. He expressed concern about the churches and obviously had some human contact because we did receive his letters to the seven churches. He had not chosen to become an island recluse. "No man is an island," the poet John Dunne wrote. To that I would add, "No man should habitually sport alone."

King David was no boater, but he was an outdoorsman who, before he became royalty, enjoyed his time tending the sheep on the mountainside. Later in life, he fled from King Saul's death threats and hid alone in the caves. At this point, David did not enjoy his return to nature. He was a fugitive, cold and hungry and lonely. Many of the psalms were written during this period of wilderness exile as David poured out his fears and frustrations, almost to the point of desperation. In reading David's laments, I can think of only two things that sustained him during those trials: (1) his trust in God, and (2) the knowledge that Jonathan, the son of his enemy Saul, was still his faithful friend. Jonathan had intervened once before and saved David from Saul's wrath. Jonathan had said to David, " 'Whatever you want me to do, I'll do for you' " (1 Samuel 20:4). With a friend like that, it is possible to walk bravely through the shadows. Even though Jonathan was not physically with David in his "hideout," he was with David in his heart. First Samuel 18:1 reports that "Jonathan became one in spirit with David, and he loved him as himself."

Over time, true friendships of that kind no longer require physical presence. One of my best friends lives hundreds of miles away; but the knowledge that he is, and always will be, like a brother to me is a source of great comfort and strength. Absentee friendships work, however, only after years of spending time together. Each time you invite a buddy to join you on a camping trip or to the golf course or in the fishing boat, you are investing in the friendship bank for future days. If a time comes when, because of physical disability, you are unable to carry golf bags together or launch the bass boat, you will still be able to pick up the phone and call your "Jonathan."

TODAY'S PRAYER:

*Dear Jesus, thank You for calling me "friend." Forgive me for taking my friendships for granted. Help me be more mindful of the importance of maintaining strong, deep relationships. Help me show love and forgiveness to my friends the way You have shown love and mercy to me. Amen.*

## CHAPTER 23:

# GOD AND THE FISHERMEN: BACK TO FISHING

TODAY'S SCRIPTURE:

*As Jesus walked beside the Sea of Galilee,*

*he saw Simon and his brother Andrew casting a net into the*

*lake, for they were fishermen. "Come, follow me,"*

*Jesus said, "and I will make you fishers of men."*

*At once they left their nets and followed him.*

MARK 1:16–18

# Called and Hooked

Jesus went neither to the temple nor the university to recruit His top twelve followers. The first two disciples He called were simply fishermen. Simon Peter and his brother Andrew were common, unaccomplished men—maybe not even very good at fishing (see Luke 5:5)! Jesus called them while walking among the fishing boats on the Galilean shore. He didn't call them by saying, "Come, I'll make you famous and rich, and everyone will love you." He said, "Come, follow me, and I will make you fishers of men." That "hooked them," and they answered His call.

Pastors often talk about "the call to preach" as if there had been a literal shout from God, yet most preachers have never heard God speak aloud. The "call" is more like a strong sense of intuition, confirmed by the church. I sensed my "call" to serve Christ when I was sitting under a tree by Fish River. To help me make the right choice, God wordlessly called me, right then in the woods, to follow Christ's way. If I had heard God's audible voice—which I didn't—it would have still been less of a miracle than the fact that God was even seeking me out in the first place. I had left God and, like the famous Prodigal Son, had run toward "riotous living" for years. I had not been looking for Jesus. However, as soon as I had the passing thought of changing my life's direction, there was

God, not just waiting for me but eagerly calling me back! Yes, I found myself smack-dab in the middle of a modern parable of a prodigal. Like the father in the Parable of the Prodigal Son, God had come to meet me, running to catch the repentant renegade, the rebel, the returning runaway.

# FISHING FOR BUNNIES

Which leads to one more fish tale. Well, it starts out as a bunny tale. *Runaway Bunny,* by Margaret Wise Brown, is one of my top five favorite children's books. It's the story of a baby bunny whose feelings get hurt and who, as many children do, threatens to run away from home. His loving mother bunny assures him that she would chase after him. So then he begins to invent clever scenarios in which he might escape her loving arms. "If you run after me," whines the little bunny, "I will become a fish. . .and I will swim away from you." To which his mother calmly replies, "If you become a fish. . .I will become a fisherman and I will fish for you."[3] The next page shows an exquisite illustration (by Clement Hurd) of the mother bunny dressed in wading boots, a net in one hand and a fishing pole in the other— with a carrot for bait!

This is a heartwarming depiction of parental love. More than that, it's a picture of the gospel. The good news is that God is much like "Mother Bunny," willing to do anything, become anything, to call back runaway children. Perhaps this is why the story of the Prodigal Son is such a popular parable. It gives us a refreshing image of God. In mythology and ancient pagan religions, the gods are wrathful, cold, mighty tyrants.

To many Americans today, God is a vague "force," an impersonal energy found in crystals or Ouija boards, but not in the face of Christ. Jesus tells us of a God who is intimately involved in the lives of humans, who cares for us like a family member, and who longs for us to return to His love—even if we have rebelled. Like Mother Bunny or like an anxious father, God calls His lost children home.

Christ called the fishermen of Galilee and told them that they could be "fishers of men." He was calling them to be "Christians," which means to be "like Christ." And Christ is first and foremost a fisherman Himself—a fisher of men, that is. He walks upon the waters to assist us when we get in over our heads. He reaches out His hand to the sinking man with weak faith and pulls him to safety. He reels in the lost and emotionally drowning woman and brings her aboard. He casts His net of love over all of us. We are God's prize catch!

### Today's Prayer:

*Christ our Redeemer, I thank You for not giving up on me, for waiting on me, for calling me. Help me hear Your call to discipleship, that I might humbly assist You in the task of "fishing" for the lost. Amen.*

CHAPTER 24:

# SINKING BOATS AND A TITANIC QUESTION

TODAY'S SCRIPTURE:

*But when [Peter] saw the wind, he was afraid and, begin-*
*ning to sink, cried out, "Lord, save me!" Immediately Jesus*
*reached out his hand and caught him.*

MATTHEW 14:30–31

# THE GREAT EQUALIZER

The word "titanic" is a synonym for "gargantuan." *Titanic* is one of the biggest-budgeted and best-selling movies of all time, based on the true story of the ill-fated ship. It was a great film with stunning special effects, marred by teen sex and violence. Nevertheless, the larger events portrayed in the movie and in the real historical incident teach us powerful lessons about which things are most important in life.

With the sinking of the *Titanic*, the rich and the poor found themselves equaled and humbled by freezing waters. Reportedly, in those last moments as the ship sank, millionaires grabbed up apples and oranges rather than gold and diamonds. The impending peril, the unexpected intrusion of death, instantly caused a reevaluation of priorities. A flask of water became more valuable than a strand of pearls. That big event in history prompts a question of *titanic* proportions: What really matters in life?

From my earliest memories, I have been fascinated with boats and ships. I would be thrilled to travel back in time to cruise on the *Titanic*, at least until it hit the iceberg! The first luxury I bought as an adult was a boat, even knowing that boats do have a bad habit of sinking. I saw this first-hand once at a boat launch. While waiting my turn at the ramp, I watched as two young fellows unwinched their boat from its trailer into the river and maneuvered it to the nearby dock. I held the mooring rope for them as they tried to start their engine. It made odd sounds and failed to crank, and I could see from their puzzled looks they knew nothing about boat motors. The novices were grateful for my offer to come aboard and help, confessing that they had just that day purchased the boat and this was their maiden voyage. After lifting the engine compartment hood, I immediately discovered the problem—an engine halfway under water! More water was streaming in from the stern. I asked with a smile, "Did you guys put in the drain plug before you launched her?"

They looked at each other, looked back at me, and—I swear this is true—said, "What's a drain plug?" We quickly scrambled to get the boat back on the trailer and managed to salvage it from the waters before it became a "titanic" disaster.

## OVER THEIR HEADS

That episode is a parable of spiritual immaturity, exemplified by a lack of patience. The apostle Peter was not the first nor the last impatient person to launch impulsively into the water without having made proper preparations. That's where we get the phrase "in over his head." Without adequate knowledge of how to stay afloat, it's no wonder that so many people find themselves quickly sinking in life's woes of divorce, alcoholism, drug abuse, gambling addiction, or "drowning in debt" due to a lack of discipline. Thankfully, Jesus will lift us out of our sinking situations just as He did for Peter. But it would be wiser to avoid getting in over our heads in the first place. Spiritual maturity requires patient preparation, study, and discipline, as well as a willingness to make hard choices and right decisions. I pray that this devotional book might be the beginning of a new journey on the road of spiritual discipline for some readers.

# Dead in the Water

Speaking of boats, another true story: Approaching forty, Jerry yearned for a speedboat. He put it off because his family had more pressing expenses and needs. Then he read an obituary of a high school classmate named Ted. Jerry was certain Ted's death was a sign that life is too short. So Jerry purchased an expensive boat that very weekend. Days later another former classmate telephoned Jerry and commented, "It sure was a sad thing, Ted getting killed in that boating accident." That's what you call irony! Death, even the threat of death, has a powerful way of changing our priorities.

Sadly, this world's priorities seem to be money and material objects. If you have "bought into" that philosophy, perhaps you should ask the survivors of the *Titanic* about what matters in life. Oranges trump diamonds. In the face of death, values are reshuffled.

It's easy to think, "When I have enough money put away, *someday* I'll be able to enjoy life. *Someday* I'll be able to enjoy my family. *Someday* I'll have time to do more volunteer work." But *somehow* we keep putting off *someday*. We had best get our priorities straight today, for tomorrow may not come.

# FIRST THINGS FIRST

This is what Jesus was teaching in the famous parable of the foolish man who, after accumulating great wealth, said, " '[Now I will] take life easy; eat, drink and be merry.' " In Luke 12:20, Jesus said, " 'This very night your life will be demanded from you. Then who will get what you have prepared for yourself?' " And in verses 29–31, Jesus concluded, " 'Do not set your heart on what you will eat or drink; do not worry about it. . . . Your Father knows that you need them. But seek his kingdom, and these things will be given to you as well.' "

Can you hear that? Jesus is not forbidding the pleasures and necessities of life. Jesus wants you to have a joyful life. No, the problem with the fool was that he set his heart on temporary things and not on the eternal kingdom of God. We are talking about more than money here. This is an issue of priorities and of what you give your heart and life to. Asking the "titanic" question "What matters most to you?" is a life and death exercise. The truth be told, our lives *always* hang in the balance. Four thin minutes without oxygen to the brain and this life ends.

In acknowledging our frail mortality, we should become more reliant upon God. If you carry away nothing else from this book, hear this great truth: The more dependent you are upon God, the more content you will be. If you set your heart upon God's kingdom, you will be a better person.

Christ calls us to awaken to life, love, and eternity. Be more mindful of the spiritual. Look for God's handiwork in the beauty of nature and God's hand in the miracle of your own life and family. Change priorities. Let the divine, the eternal, and the spiritual come first. Let it penetrate all that we are and all that we do. The spiritual will greatly outlast our jet skis and bass boats. Why, then, do we not place it first? Why, then, is Christ not central? After all, it is our *life in Christ* that really matters. I pray you will never have a "titanic" disaster in your life—but if you ever do find yourself sinking, drowning in sin and sorrow, toil and trouble, look to the One who can walk on the water and whose love can lift you up.

TODAY'S PRAYER:

*O Lord of Love, lift me up from the depths to which I have fallen. Fill my heart with a longing for Your love and my mind with a yearning for Your kingdom. Guide me in reordering my priorities in life. Show me how Your Spirit can work in every aspect of my work and play that I might grow in spiritual maturity. In Jesus' name. Amen.*

# CHAPTER 25:

# THE
# FINAL
# CHAPTER?

TODAY'S SCRIPTURE:

*The earth is the LORD's, and everything in it, the world,*

*and all who live in it; for he founded it upon the seas*

*and established it upon the waters.*

PSALM 24:1–2

# Real Life

We had planted a small sapling in our backyard, probably too late, too close to autumn. The leaves quickly fell off of it. The tree—which is a generous word for it, since it more closely resembled a single small stick pointing up from the ground—stood dormant through the wind and snow of winter. Spring came, and all the other trees and flowers in our yard bloomed. . .but not the sapling. Not a leaf, not even a bud. Another month went by, and I was convinced that the tree had not survived the transplant. I resolved that the next time I ran the mower, I would just mow down the little stalk. A week later, before I cranked the mower, I gave it one more look and noticed two buds! Another week passed, and two leaves had unfolded. Despite that feeble start, the tree eventually took hold, growing taller and leafier and stronger.

This is the message nature sends us again and again: Life is resilient. Death wins some battles, but death never wins the war. Life will triumph over extinction.

Several chapters of this book deal with the topic of death. Although this chapter is entitled "The Final Chapter?" it is not about death. It is about life and resurrection. The life we lead in this world is only a prologue for a greater story to come. I do not like to call it the "Afterlife," for our current life is the "Pre-Life" and life in heaven is the "REAL Life." If we trust in God's love and grace, there will be no final chapter.

# THROUGH A GLASS DIMLY

In our fallen, sinful condition, we don't see things so clearly; and we're especially blind to the reality of eternal life. St. Paul had a vision of heaven, yet he still cautioned in 1 Corinthians 2:9 that " 'no eye has seen, no ear has heard, no mind has conceived what God has prepared for those who love him.' " Life beyond this veil of tears is grander than we can imagine. Nevertheless, it is healthy to try. It's good to get glimpses of the coming kingdom that we might keep our "eyes on the prize."

I have suggested that you can encounter God anywhere, in the church pew and in the bass boat. But when it comes to getting glimpses of heaven and the glories of eternal life, you really must go outdoors. Eternity can be glimpsed in a Rocky Mountain blue sky or just beyond the horizon of the turquoise gulf waters; but I've never seen it in a Sunday sermon. And this is a preacher talking!

# Nature's Object Lesson

Our Creator made our minds finite, but God placed us in an infinite universe. We are floating in eternity. Nature, overflowing with life and beauty, points to the concept of resurrection. On Easter Sundays, I use nature's object lessons to teach children. Adults would do well to go outside, take a wide-eyed look at nature, and learn the lessons firsthand. Here are some examples:

- We had our driveway paved with thick, hot, black asphalt. Two weeks later, a pristine white mushroom pushed its way up through the pavement and spread out its dome. The mushroom was as soft as tissue, while the asphalt was hard as rock. I call that miraculous—another reminder that life is amazingly resilient.

- Consider the power hidden in a seed. Sit under a mighty oak tree, one of those hundred-year-old majesties whose limbs stretch out forty feet in all directions, big as a mansion. Pick up an acorn. That oak came from just such a tiny start. Do you still have trouble envisioning life after death? Try again: A scientist took a grain of wheat found inside an Egyptian pyramid, where it had been entombed for thousands of years. He gave the wheat seed water, soil, and sunlight; and within a day, it germinated, came back to life.

- The classic illustration is the caterpillar who turns into a butterfly, with the cocoon (actually a chrysalis) as a symbol of the tomb and death. I can share a personal experience with this. My daughter Melissa found a large cocoon. Thinking I could use the object lesson on her, I said to her: "Let's take this into the house and eventually you will see a butterfly or moth emerge from it. Think of the caterpillar as a human in this life— dumb, ugly, and sluggish, eating and sleeping until it gets old and tired. It goes into its tomb— the cocoon—and falls asleep. To all outside observation, it is dead. But in silence, it changes. Then, after time passes, it slowly emerges from the cocoon, a beautiful new creature with angelic wings, and flies away into eternity. That is kind of how I imagine death and resurrection will be for us." So months of winter went by and we forgot about the cocoon. As Easter Sunday approached, I remembered it. The cocoon was lifeless. "Melissa, spring is here and the moth has not hatched out. When I shake it, there is no movement inside. It even sounds dried up. I'm afraid it died." So much for the object lesson.

The month of May came. I was called to the hospital room of Betty Miller, who had been a great spiritual leader in our church until stricken with a debilitating disease. Now she was dying before her time. As I prayed at her bedside, she slipped away into that next and better place. I went to sleep with a heavy heart that night.

In the middle of the night, I was awakened by a *tap, tap, tapping* on the window. A burglar? Adrenaline flowing, I flipped on the light switch and to my shock discovered the source of the tapping. A large, gorgeous Polyphemus moth was banging repeatedly against the window, trying to get out to the full moon, I suppose. I let it loose and watched it fly off into the night. *How did such a large moth get in the house?* I wondered. And then it hit me. I ran and found the cocoon. Empty. Once again, my faith in life over death had been too small.

Two days later, we had the funeral for Betty Miller. In my funeral message, I shared the story of the resurrected moth. From the stunned looks on their faces, I figured the family understood the symbolism of a "dead" caterpillar coming to life as a moth on the same day that Betty took flight from this world. But it was more than that. A family member then told us, in their part of the eulogy, that Betty loved butterflies—they were her "trademark," her favorite symbol of faith in God's gift of eternal life. So much so that, without knowing I would be using the metaphor, the family had purchased a box of live butterflies to release at the graveside. As twenty-four beautiful butterflies flew off into the sky, we knew that God had sent us a miraculous reassurance of resurrection.

# A NEW STORY BEGINS

The miracle of resurrection is hard for our minds to grasp. Myths and fairy tales across the centuries have at once helped us imagine it while making it seem so fantastical as to be something only found in, well, fairy tales! In this world, we also have difficulty imagining a story without an end. Our narratives have a beginning, middle, and an end. And we view our lives like stories. When we reach retirement age, we view that as a final chapter, or worse, an epilogue. Even if our life story lasts for eighty or ninety years, we still tend to be shortsighted, thinking short term relative to eternity. If we truly believe in resurrection and eternal life, we should understand that this life is only a prologue; and the real, never-ending story just barely begins when the coroner signs off.

C. S. Lewis concluded his famous children's classic *The Last Battle*, of the Chronicles of Narnia series, with appropriate words to close any book. His characters had all died. . .more than that, they were all entering heaven. "And for us this is the end of all the stories. . . . But for them it was only the beginning of the real story. All their life in this world. . .had only been the cover and the title page: now at last they were beginning Chapter One of the Great Story which no one on earth has read: which goes on forever:

in which every chapter is better than the one before."

As I said, there is no final chapter. Close this book, open your door, and go outdoors with God. Eternity is waiting.

# SOURCES

*American Heritage Dictionary, The.* Boston: Houghton Mifflin Co., 1992.

Baum, L. Frank. *The Wizard of Oz.* New York: George Hill Co., 1900.

Brown, Margaret Wise. *Runaway Bunny.* New York: Harper and Row, 1970.

Fulghum, Robert. *All I Really Need to Know I Learned in Kindergarten.* New York: Villard Books, 1990.

Lewis, C. S. *The Great Divorce.* San Francisco: Harper, 2001.

_____. The Chronicles of Narnia: *The Last Battle.* New York: HarperCollins, 1994.

Maclean, Norman. *A River Runs Through It.* Chicago: University of Chicago Press, 1976.

Sweet, Leonard. *The Jesus Prescription for a Healthy Life.* Nashville: Abingdon Press, 1996.

----

[1] Name and exact details have been changed, but the story is true.

[2] Leonard Sweet, *The Jesus Prescription for a Healthy Life* (Nashville: Abingdon Press, 1996), pp. 40–41.

[3] Margaret Wise Brown, *Runaway Bunny* (New York: Harper and Row, 1970).

# About the Author

The Reverend Doctor Lance Moore is a former rock guitarist, now pastor of First United Methodist Church of Monroeville, Alabama. He and his wife, Diana, have two children: Melissa and Amanda. He is coauthor of the book *Firm Foundations: An Architect and a Pastor Guide Your Church Construction.*

# If you enjoyed

*Outdoors with God*
be sure to check out the following books,
also available from Barbour Publishing, Inc.

*My Utmost for His Highest*
ISBN 1-57748-914-4
Hardback, 288 pages, $9.97

*Prayers & Promises for Men*
ISBN 1-58660-833-9
Printed Leatherette, 224 pages, $4.97

*Prayers & Promises for Women*
ISBN 1-58660-832-0
Printed Leatherette, 224 pages, $4.97

*Come Away My Beloved*
ISBN 1-58660-576-3
Hardback, 256 pages, $12.97

Available wherever books are sold.